ONE
COMPA

ONE'S COMPANY

A PRACTICAL GUIDE TO ENJOYING YOUR INDEPENDENCE

Lynn Underwood

Ashford
Southampton
1989

Published by Ashford
1 Church Road
Shedfield
Hampshire SO3 2HW

British Library Cataloguing in Publication Data

Underwood, Lynn
    One's company: a practical guide to enjoying your independence
    1. Living alone – Manuals
    I. Title
    306.8′8

    ISBN 1-85253-102-9 (Hardback)
    ISBN 1-85253-101-0 (Paperback)

Typeset by Consort Art Graphics, Exeter, Devon, England
Printed in Great Britain by BPCC Wheatons Ltd, Exeter

Contents

Preface   7
Acknowledgements   9

1 · How to have a life, not an existence   11
   Life is what you make it   13
   The breakthrough   16
   The hermit complex   17
   Banishing anxieties   18

2 · The place where you live   22
   Whether or not to move   22
   The choice of area   23
   Assessing your chosen area   24
   The home itself   27
   Renting a property   36
   Buying a home   38
   Organising the move   43

3 · Your home is your castle   47
   Security is the first priority   47
   Personal safety inside the home   51
   Avoiding accidents in the home   54
   Making yourself comfortable   58
   The art of gracious living   62
   Now put up your feet and indulge yourself   65

4 · Managing money   67
   Is enough money coming in?   67
   Assessing the incomings and outgoings   76
   Banking arrangements   88
   Dealing with debt   90

5 · Eating for one – or more   94
   The freezer   95
   Your store cupboard   97
   Buying fresh produce   99
   Useful cooking aids   100
   Feeding guests   101

6 · Anything but lonely   105
    Company in your home   105
    Going out   107

7 · Looking after yourself   116
    Taking good care of yourself   116
    First aid in the home   125
    Hypothermia   129

8 · Taking a break   130
    The options   130
    Your health and safety abroad   135
    Preparing for your holiday   137

9 · Sharing your space   139
    Keeping pets   139
    Animal intruders   142
    Having visitors   145

Useful Names and Addresses   149
Useful Leaflets   152
Useful Books   156
Index   159

Preface

The idea for this book arose gradually – partly from my own experiences of living alone and partly from my experiences of other people living alone, particularly the elderly.

When I was in my mid twenties I left the parental home for the second time and set myself up in a flat in South London. I loved the flat: it was large and roomy, with a perfect view over a large garden and some playing fields. I loved my solitary state too. For the first time in my life I was organised (even houseproud!) and relished the fact that I could eat when I liked; have a bath at midnight; lie in bed at weekends; watch my favourite programmes on television – all without comment from anyone else.

The most important thing about my home, though, was that it was safe. In fact, that was one of the major selling points put forward by the estate agent. It was on the second floor, approached by an open staircase which was well lit. It was on a main road, close to a police station. In short, it was burglar-proof. The ideal home for a single girl. It was also within walking distance of two railway stations, there was a laundrette opposite the door, and a bus stop outside the door, which made the short trip into the nearest shopping centre very easy. I wish that I could claim that I had considered all these factors with care when I took over the flat, but I did not, I was merely lucky.

The idea for a book about living alone really crystallised when I was asked by a property magazine to write an article about viewing and choosing a home. I decided to approach it from the point of view of the single person, of any age, and write about the careful selection of a home that was safe, secure and had all the amenities at hand. The article was a success and drew considerable response from the magazine's readers, many of whom were single and felt that most articles that dealt with the home automatically assumed that home-buyers were couples.

During the course of writing the article I had researched the statistics pertaining to the number of people who lived alone and was astonished. There was a large section of the population that was not being catered for in any of the major bookshops. I found plenty of books and magazines about marriage and babies, some about retirement, some about teenagehood, but nothing about the important stage in life experienced by practically everybody at one time or another – being single. Of course, many magazines cater for the 'swinging singles' – telling the readers how to have a great social life – but even they seemed to regard the single state as a temporary misfortune and spend most of their time offering suggestions as to how one could share one's life.

It seemed to me that a positive tone was needed here. Many people enjoy living alone and there is nothing wrong with them. Many people find themselves living alone later in life and should be encouraged to enjoy it, but are not. True, I came across some organisations, such as CRUSE (The National Organisation for the Widowed and their Children), that help people overcome bereavement and attain self-sufficiency, and the various bodies that assist the elderly naturally recognise that the imbalance of the sexes beyond a certain age means that not everyone can aspire to being part of a couple in their later years, but, in the main, Victorian attitudes still prevailed. Phrases like 'on the shelf' were still around while 'confirmed bachelor', 'spinster', 'career girl', 'widow' and 'widower' were used in the same vein as words like 'monk' or 'nun' and 'hermit'.

I felt that this was wrong. Living alone is a privilege, not a sentence. So I set about writing this book in the hope that it would give a fillip to a very neglected and under-rated section of our society.

Acknowledgements

I should like to thank the following organisations for their assistance in supplying information for this book:

Abbey National Building Society; Age Concern; Alliance Leicester Building Society; Anchor Housing Trust; Arthritis Care; The Association of British Travel Agents Ltd; Banking Information Service; The Bethlem Royal Hospital; Bradford & Bingley Building Society; The British Security Industry Association; The Building Societies Association; The Carr-Gomm Society; Confederation Life Insurance Co.; Counsel and Care for the Elderly; Coventry Building Society; Crisis at Christmas; CRUSE; Commercial Union Assurance Co. plc; Disabled Living Foundation; The Family Welfare Association; Gateway Building Society; General Accident Fire & Life Assurance Corporation plc; Guardian Royal Exchange; Halifax Building Society; The Joseph Rowntree Trust; The Leamington Spa Building Society; Leeds Permanent Building Society; Lloyds Bank; The Mental After-Care Association; Midland Bank plc; The National Association of Estate Agents; National Association for Mental Health; The National Council of Women of Great Britain; National Westminster Bank; Nationwide Anglia Building Society; Price Waterhouse; The Royal Bank of Scotland plc; Royal Insurance (UK) Ltd; Royal Life Insurance Ltd; Royal Society for the Prevention of Cruelty to Animals; The Salvation Army; Sun Alliance Insurance Group; Sun Life Assurance Society plc; Women's Royal Voluntary Service; Woolwich Equitable Building Society; and the Yorkshire Bank.

1·HOW TO HAVE A LIFE, NOT AN EXISTENCE

When one lives alone, the world seems to be made up of couples, but, in fact, it is not. In the United Kingdom, almost one-third of the population lives alone – that is around twenty million people – hardly a minority group. What is more, owing to various factors, the number of people living alone is growing.

People live by themselves temporarily or permanently, by choice or by chance. They may start out their adult life living alone, spend some of their middle years living alone, or end their days living alone. But what should be a happy and fulfilling experience all too often is not. This book is about achieving the most from that time of your life, whenever it occurs. It is about eliminating regrets, fears and anxieties and injecting a positive quality into time spent without other people.

I have often played host to married friends who bemoan their lack of privacy, or express their desire to be able to put themselves first, once in a while, instead of their partner, parent(s), children or grandchildren. That is not to say, however, that this book is meant to praise living alone in preference to sharing your life. There is nothing wrong in living alone or in hoping that one day you will share your life or, in the case of those who are divorced or bereaved, share your life again. But such hopes should not overshadow any time alone to the extent that they lead to depression and lack of self appreciation. No one should waste the potential for a good life by wishing that things were different.

Living alone does not mean solitary confinement. Friends

and neighbours are not the prerogative of couples. Rather, it is the single person who is in the position to balance a social life and complete privacy. Being healthy and happy is the aim of the single person as well as everyone else. They have an equal right not to dread going to bed alone, or waking up alone; there need be no loneliness on quiet Sundays.

There are many different reasons for being alone and equally different needs to be considered for the people who find themselves in this position. Many people find that they live alone through no plan or design. Life just has not provided them with a partner and so they wander on through their thirties and forties, still living alone and gradually accepting the situation.

Of course, a number of people start their period of being alone in some distress. Divorce or bereavement means that loneliness and grief play a large part in their life for some time. But even if this is your situation it is important to establish some degree of self-sufficiency from the outset to help you become stronger and happier eventually.

The hardest task of all may be that of people choosing to live alone who are either disabled or who have been members of an institution. Disabled people, in particular, often have a greater degree of self-sufficiency than many able-bodied people however. Moreover, both of these groups, while they will need a great deal of outside support in the initial stages, have perhaps more reason to welcome the independence and privacy a single lifestyle gives them than anyone else. Relishing the state is half the battle towards a good life, for everyone.

Others, students or young people working away from their family home, start out a life alone full of hope, anticipation and excitement. But the heady joy of escaping from the routine and demands of one's family can soon evaporate into anxiety and loneliness.

Some adults make the choice to live on their own after they have tried various shared living arrangements and discovered that they prefer to be in control of their own life and make their own rules. Theirs is a perfectly good decision that need only become a problem if at a later stage they find that it has become too difficult to share their life and a potential relationship disintegrates through their selfishness.

Achieving total independence without loneliness or self absorption is a tricky business for everyone. Like everything else in life that is worth having it requires some effort and self discipline. To create a quality of life that is admired by all your friends who do not live alone, demands thought, planning, perseverance and a degree of practicality, although in essence all of this is determined by the will to live rather than merely exist.

LIFE IS WHAT YOU MAKE IT

Whatever the situation in which you find yourself living alone; whether your husband or wife has left you or the children have left home; whether your husband or wife or elderly parent has died or your flatmate has left; whether you are starting college or a new job or have just decided to leave the family home, you must accept and make the very best of your new life.

Bereaved and divorced

The trauma of a bereavement or divorce is devastating. People in these tragic circumstances have to come to terms with their sense of loss before they can come to terms with, and learn to enjoy, living alone.

The first thing is to admit that, temporarily, you need support and help. Medication is not always the right resource in times of distress, but there are certain situations that are so terrible that you will need something to help you through the first few months. Not tranquillisers – no one benefits from making their life into a cotton wool ball. Many anti-depressants are non-addictive and your doctor will advise you on this. The fact is that you may need something to help you cope, sleep and carry on with your life. You will feel

13

totally alone because you have relied on someone to do things with you and for you for some time. But you can do these things yourself. If there is something you cannot do, you can ask a friend to help or pay someone to do it for you. Hold on to that thought and try not to panic. You can do anything – eventually. You will be able to cope.

ORGANISATIONS

CRUSE (The National Organisation for the Widowed and their Children), and other organisations like it, provide support and a valuable shoulder to cry on when you do not know what to do. Apart from the support groups that CRUSE runs, it also produces a large range of literature about the problems of bereavement and it provides practical help in dealing with paperwork and other matters that a bereaved person may never have dealt with before.

THE NATIONAL MARRIAGE GUIDANCE COUNCIL (now called RELATE) recognised a long time ago that the fabric of society has changed and one of the reasons for the organisation's change of name is that it now deals with all personal crisis situations. It publishes a particularly useful book called *Alone Again – Help for the Divorced, Separated and Bereaved*, which gives practical advice and lists other support agencies.

AGE CONCERN publishes another useful book called *Survival Guide for Widows*, which again lists other organisations who will help.

THE SAMARITANS, of course, are always there on the end of the phone to listen and help. Please do not think that only suicidal people ring up the Samaritans. Many of us sometimes need to talk through our anxieties with someone other than a friend and the Samaritans are always glad to listen.

Even some of the financial institutions have begun to recognise that those who are suddenly on their own through bereavement, divorce or separation, are special customers who need help.

CU Life (Commercial Assurance) produces an excellent booklet called *Coping on Your Own*, which is an easy-to-understand guide to financial matters. The Halifax Building Society has also produced a booklet called *Home Help for Widows*, which has been compiled in conjunction with the National Association for Widows and gives practical advice on property matters.

There are many groups, much literature, and a great deal of help available for the widowed or divorced – so much that to go into the subject in detail would require another book.

Disabled

The disabled who choose to strike out on their own can, of course, turn to their local social services department for help and advice. There are many housing associations who now actively cater for the independent disabled.

ORGANISATIONS

DISABLED LIVING FOUNDATION AND RADAR (*Royal Association for Disability and Rehabilitation*) produce catalogues of aids for the disabled, to make life easier.

MIND (*the National Association for Mental Health*) provides a positive approach to those seeking an independent lifestyle after a period in an institution and has helped many.

At the moment, it is the policy within our community to help as many people as possible achieve an independent life outside of an institution. There should therefore be plenty of advice and practical help at a local level, via the social services departments and the medical profession.

Whatever the reason for living alone the main enemy everyone has to face is depression.

Young people

For the young person starting out alone there will be moments of panic – phone calls home, and moments of miserable isolation when you do not know what to do, either practically or emotionally. You will learn to cope. You are not failing – everyone has these crises, whatever age they are.

THE BREAKTHROUGH

Everyone who lives alone makes the breakthrough when they realise that living alone is not a prison sentence or a state to be endured. One day you will wake up (it may be a nice sunny Sunday morning) and you will luxuriate in the fact that you can do anything that you want to do – anything that takes your fancy – and there is no one else to consider. A divorced friend of mine said that it took her about a year to reach the breakthrough. She said that she woke up one day and did not feel lost or depressed, did not wonder what she was going to do with herself or reach for the phone to try and summon up some company. She just sat over a leisurely breakfast and planned her day, and never looked back after that.

Another friend of mine, a man who spent most of his adult life looking after his elderly parents until they both died within a year of each other, came home from work one evening and suddenly realised that he could go to the cinema and have a meal out without worrying about anyone else. For ten months after his father's death he had unquestioningly taken the same train home, cooked a meal to be eaten at 7.30 (as he had always done when his parents were alive), watched television, made a cup of tea at 9.30 (as he had done when his parents were alive), and gone to bed. His breakthrough was sudden and without apparent reason. He simply demolished the lifelong routine and began to build his own life.

The breakthrough for the young person who has left their family home is different. It may take the form of actually saying 'No' to a hectic social life. When I first left home and lived on my own, I gorged myself on an endless round of late night parties and visits to newly-found friends which lasted until the early hours of the morning. The exhilaration of not having to account for my movements to my parents went to my head. Then, after about three months, I had got it all out of my system I suppose, and I actually turned down an invitation to a party in favour of staying in and washing some clothes! I had begun to desire some balance in my life and after that my socialising was toned down and my private moments stepped up.

Of course, not all young people leave home to a whirl of social activity. The ones who leave to go to college or to live in some kind of hostel attached to a place of work, will eventually be embraced into an active social life by their peers. But many young people leave home to work, and live, in another town or even country, far away from their schoolday friends and possibly living in an isolated situation. For these people, homesickness can be terrible. Depression and loneliness will descend after the first few days of nervous euphoria. It is no consolation to say that it will pass. For some, homesickness is so bad during the first few months that they have no alternative but to go back home again.

First of all, one must recognise that homesickness is natural. You have left a place where you are loved and accepted and have come into a strange environment where you don't belong to a family unit anymore. The workplace, or place of study, exerts its own pressures on you and the fear of failure in those first few weeks just adds to your sense of isolation.

The breakthrough comes when acceptance and relaxation come. It may be during your first week at work when a colleague asks you to join him or her in a group activity, such as a drink after work with friends. It may be that you receive praise for a piece of work well done, and suddenly you feel that you made the right decision to leave the family home and strike out on your own.

THE HERMIT COMPLEX

It is an ideal situation, when living alone, that you should enjoy your own company, but you should also balance this with forays into the outside world, otherwise solitude becomes loneliness and seclusion becomes a state of imprisonment.

If you have no social life or circle of friends when you start your single lifestyle then it requires more effort on your part. It is worth making the effort to involve yourself with other people, you do not necessarily have to share your home with them.

Without social interaction we begin to see life's problems out of proportion. We need other people to talk to about our ideas, fears and hopes. MIND realised this a long time ago. I once visited a local MIND centre which was a day and short-term residential centre for people who had been in institutions with mental illness. The co-ordinator told me that many people who had come to therapy groups for anxieties or depressions were now volunteer workers. It was her firm belief that the quickest way to achieve mental health was to absorb oneself in the problems of others and, in this particular centre, it seemed to have worked.

One danger of taking the downward spiral of self-imposed isolation is agoraphobia, the fear of being away from the security of the home. It is estimated that approximately 500,000 adults in Great Britain suffer from agoraphobia to some extent. Women are particularly at risk, the majority of agoraphobics are women in the 18–35 age group. The Institute of Psychiatry at the Royal Bethlem and Maudsley Hospitals in London reports that men who live alone are more prone to alcoholism or social phobias (such as fear of meeting people).

It is too easy to lose control when one lives alone; the aim must always be to be 'alone but not lonely'. Social contact with others is a necessity and will be considered in greater depth in a later chapter.

BANISHING ANXIETIES

One of the psychiatrists I spoke to while preparing this book said that in his therapy groups for people with anxieties, he asked them to make lists of their day's worries. This served two purposes, firstly the importance of the problems was diminished when they were written down (even the most depressed person could not resist a smile when they wrote down some of their worries – somehow they looked silly on paper) and, secondly, it enabled them to delete items on the list when the problems were solved, thereby proving that most problems were capable of being solved.

Being organised can take a great deal of worry out of a single life. For example, when I first lived alone I used to be in a state of anxiety every time I left the house, for fear that I had forgotten something. I solved that problem by putting a large notice on the inside of the front door that said:

- HAVE YOU GOT YOUR KEYS?
- HAVE YOU SWITCHED OFF THE GAS FIRE AND THE OVEN?
- HAVE YOU CLOSED AND LOCKED ALL THE WINDOWS?
- HAVE YOU GOT YOUR PURSE?

It caused some mirth amongst my friends, but I noticed that several of them began to pin up similar notices in their own homes.

Shopping is a pleasure when you live alone because you do not have to do a bulk-shop every weekend as families do. You can shop meal by meal, or bit by bit. However, this has its hazards – such as forgetting to buy washing-up liquid three days in a row and not being able to do any washing up. Again, I have resorted to the pinned-up list, this time in the kitchen. Whenever I think of something that is needed, I write it on the list, and whenever I buy something, I cross it off the list.

I began to employ the list method for other things, planning my weekends for instance. I greatly enjoy sitting down on a Thursday evening to compile a list of all the pleasant and even unpleasant things I have to do, and then luxuriate in my sense of achievement on the following Sunday evening when every item on the list is ticked off.

Keeping a diary is vital when you live alone because there is no one to remind you of dental appointments or someone's birthday. I keep a pocket diary with me at all times and a calendar with spaces for writing on by the telephone. Then I make sure that both are kept up to date.

Inevitably there is a certain amount of routine in everyone's life and the person who lives alone also needs to establish some routine, no matter how tempting it may be to lead an unfettered existence, particularly if it is the first time you have lived on your own. Unless you do this you may easily find yourself persistently oversleeping, undereating or spending more than you can afford on meals out, or otherwise not achieving all you want.

Organisation does not mean martyrdom. Whether it means buying an alarm clock, making packed lunches the night before or ironing while watching television, method and routine, knowing what you have to do and finding the best way to do it will overcome most problems. Be sensible in your plans, though; there is no point in forcing yourself to do something after a hard day's work, for example.

Keeping a filing system is an important means of organisation. The value of stored documentation increases with the more things you acquire in life. Certainly, when you buy a property, the amount of paperwork accumulates. When you own a car you need to keep your driving licence, registration document, MOT certificate, and the like somewhere where you can find them every time your car needs a new tax disc. I now keep all appliance handbooks and registration cards filed away so that I can diagnose faults in, say, the food mixer, without incurring expensive servicing.

Address books are vital, not simply for friends' addresses and phone numbers but for those of anyone who might be useful. Vital names/addresses/phone numbers for any address book are:

Doctor	Local authority (rates, emergencies etc)
Dentist	Local police station
Vet	Telephone engineer

Plumber	Gas Board
Garage	Electricity Board
Taxi service	Insurance companies

Organisation means control, and control means peace of mind. Yes, it requires some self-discipline, but it is worth it in the end. Muddle, tension, anxiety, frustration do nothing to enhance the quality of your life.

2·THE PLACE WHERE YOU LIVE

This chapter is about selecting a home, but that does not mean that it is valueless if you already have a home. Circumstances may change for you. If you have been widowed, then a new home may be a good idea, once you feel like starting your life afresh.

Of course, you may not have a choice about where you live, particularly if you are a student in halls of residence, or a disabled person with special requirements. The choice may be yours in the future, though, and the right choice at the beginning can mean the difference between a happy home and misery.

WHETHER OR NOT TO MOVE

We all have to be near something – work, college, family – there are very few people who are without any ties and can genuinely live anywhere. Perhaps a retired person, with no family can honestly say 'Right, I'm selling up and moving to the Isle of Skye.' It sounds terrific, but I might pause to question the wisdom of such a move.

One of the greatest errors of our increasingly affluent society has been the 'retirement move syndrome'. A family, let us say, spend their entire life in suburbia. The children grow up and move away. The husband and wife retire from their work and immediately move down to some retirement haven in deepest Cornwall. Within two years, one of them dies, leaving the other one alone and friendless without support in a community he or she barely knows.

Understandably people want to look forward to retirement,

and for many people part of that dream is the rose-covered cottage or modern bungalow in the country or by the sea. Not only are they moving away, but often they are also moving to a place totally unsuitable for elderly people. The south coast of England was revived by estate agents from a fading, genteel holiday coastline into a supposed retirement paradise, and yet winter by the sea (whatever the summer attractions) can be savage. Even Torquay, when there is two-and-a-half feet of snow on the ground, will lose some of its appeal. Cornwall and Devon have some of the hilliest countryside in the country, and the agility of a mountain goat is needed in order to traverse it – hardly suitable for someone who is elderly, and may well become frail. You may be happiest not moving.

THE CHOICE OF AREA

For those of us who are not free to live exactly where we want picking a place to live is very, very important. The following is a checklist of the first three considerations which should be taken into account before anything else:

1. How mobile are you? Do you have a car or do you rely on public transport?
2. Do you *need* to be near to something e.g. schools, college, work, family, medical services?
3. Do you *want* to be near to something e.g. friends, theatres, swimming baths, country parks, bustling town?

Mobility

Your mobility to some extent governs the other two considerations. If you have a car then you have greater flexibility, but sometimes additional problems. For example, I live in a rural village that is prized because of its good connections with London. There are two stations within ten minutes drive from which travellers may be in London in under an hour. Neither of these stations are any use to me if my car is out of action, however, because I could not possibly walk to them. That happens to be all right for me because I do not have to commute regularly but it could be a consideration. So mobility has to be qualified. If you have a *reliable* car then you have greater flexibility whatever the situation.

If you have to rely solely on public transport then the rural life may not be such a good idea, unless everything that you have to be near is within your area.

Needing to be near to something

Obviously, you have obligations. You may have to study, attend a hospital for special treatment, go to work, be near your family. How near you have to be depends upon your mobility.

Wanting to be near to something

Everyone can relate to the problems of accommodating all their desires in the same place. There is no choice but to analyse your own needs and be honest with yourself, weighing up one 'want' against another, before you actually set out to look for a place to live. Again, your mobility may determine your ability to put certain things into your life like art galleries, theatres, etc. whilst living at a distance from them. It cannot change your environment, though, and you must decide what is most important to you.

ASSESSING YOUR CHOSEN AREA

Once you have chosen the approximate area in which you want to live and the area that fits your first criteria of need, want and mobility you must make a deeper assessment:

WHAT IS PUBLIC TRANSPORT LIKE? Even if you can drive you may not always have or have use of a car, but you will always need to reach the shops, go to the bank, to the doctor's, and so on. Young people striking out on their own for the first time frequently do not have transport and colleges or universities are not always situated in city centres. Elderly people must face the possibility of no longer being able to drive. Transport is always a prime consideration.

WHAT ARE THE LOCAL AMENITIES? You will not always want to visit the nearest metropolis for your essentials. It helps if there is a little local parade of shops that covers everything – butchers, bakers, grocers, greengrocers, in particular a pharmacy, newsagents, doctor's surgery and post office. The last four are essential. No one wants to undertake a journey of any length if they are ill, much less to have a prescription filled out. A post office is invaluable because it can also act as a bank, not only during the week, but on Saturday mornings when normal banks are usually closed. It is always wise to have a source of money close at hand for emergencies, but not wise to keep much in the house, or to rely on a neighbourhood bank if you will not be near it during banking hours.

WHERE ARE THE EMERGENCY SERVICES? It is always comforting to have hospitals, fire stations, and police close at hand so that you know that they will not have far to come if you need them. Mind you I wouldn't recommend having them next door like I did when I lived in South London. There is little comfort in being woken up at three in the morning by a fire engine proceeding to a fire.

WHAT IS THE CLIMATE LIKE? This may sound a silly question, since this book assumes that its readers are looking for a place to live in the British Isles, but it is more sensible than it sounds. Where I live at present is bounded by two rivers and is quite close to the sea. What I did not realise when I bought the house was that in the winter, and sometimes in the summer, the fog rolls thickly in and you cannot see your hand in front of your face. You should be aware of the peculiarities of the local weather before you make your mind up to live in a particular place. You may find something that will affect your decision.

ARE THERE ANY SEASONAL DISTURBANCES? Many people have viewed and bought a house in a quiet lane during the summer, only to find, in October, that the lovely field behind the house in fact belongs to a school and is filled with playing children for most of the year. Similarly, it could become an active football pitch during the winter season and your kitchen window may be sited just behind the goalmouth.

ARE THERE ANY LOCAL PROBLEMS? People who buy houses next to pubs must be prepared for the consequences. A pub is a perfectly obvious building to detect on viewing the house and even the most refined drinking place or restaurant is going to subject the surrounding properties to a certain amount of noise as people come and go, as is a large supermarket or a village hall. However attractive the decor of the bathroom or the built-in kitchen they will not obscure a local public amenity once you return to the property as an owner.

WHAT IS LIFE LIKE WHERE YOU ARE GOING? Rurality is fine, but a village without a village hall suggests a lack of social life. The local library is the place to find lists of local societies and discover what is happening in the area. Social activities are important. Even if you do not have a social life when you settle in, you will want something to do, and it is important to see if your interests are catered for within the local community. There is little point in moving to a community that does not cater for your tastes, or which does not offer interesting opportunities.

Another factor in selecting a home and a potential social life, is the predominant age of the community that you have selected. Many new towns on the fringe of the affluent south-east are so heavily populated by young married couples that they simply do not cater for retired people in any of their social activities; similarly, you may be pushed to find an under-30s' club in a retirement village on the south coast.

ARE THERE ANY BUILDING PROJECTS IN HAND IN THE AREA? Your solicitor will do a local search if you buy a property, but you may be renting in which case no one will do a search for you. You will have to go to the local council offices yourself to find out what plans are on the horizon. If you do not, you may move into a home only to find, three months later, that the road outside your flat is being widened into a motorway, or an uninterrupted view over woodlands is to be rudely interrupted by the erection of a new housing estate.

IS THE AREA SAFE? Those who live alone perhaps need to be especially secure from harm coming and going from their home. This applies to both men and women, for although women are often the victims of violent street crime, men are also mugged just as easily, particularly elderly men. Rural areas tend to be safer than urban areas, but, nevertheless, you need to apply the same judgement wherever you choose to live. Is the area well lit and well policed? Do you have to cross lonely stretches of ground between your home and the bus stop or railway station? The newspapers are sadly filled with instances of girls being assaulted or murdered in broad daylight on lonely walks home. Do you have to pass potential trouble spots such as discos or pubs in order to reach your front door? Having to negotiate rowdy drunks is no laughing matter. Is the area prone to burglaries? Go to the library and read a year's worth of back copies of the local newspapers, that should tell you what you need to know.

THE HOME ITSELF

When you are satisfied that the area you like is, in fact, all that you hoped it would be, you can turn your attention to the actual property.

Looking for a house or flat means taking lots of details from estate agents and viewing properties if they take your fancy. Rule number one is, whether renting or buying, never to take anything out of desperation – you will only regret it. *Something* will turn up. It may take patience, but it is important to be fastidious about what sort of home you are prepared to inhabit.

Different people, naturally, have different requirements. Someone who is giving up their former marital home because of divorce or bereavement will probably be anxious not to sacrifice too greatly the lifestyle they enjoyed before. They will need space and comfort, perhaps a garden if they have always been used to one and enjoy gardening, and, above all, they will need a property that gives them some self esteem and security. Young people, in their first home, can usually accept a much lower standard, as long as it is dry and warm. The disabled and frail elderly will, of course, have special requirements and will need to select a home with a view to adaptation. Those who are single and affluent will be looking for a residence of some quality. Perhaps with their greater freedom they are most easily blinded by the options and may forget to take account of the special needs of those who live alone.

Security

Renting or buying a safe home is the number one priority. It does not matter how beautiful the decor, or how ravishing the garden: if it is not safe and secure you should not move in.

In an urban environment, basement flats are not advisable for the single dweller. The police report that over 40 per cent of burglaries of urban dwellings are break-ins to basement flats. They are easily accessible and hidden from view. They also have the disadvantage of being dark and prone to damp, and are seemingly tempting places to deposit litter, or worse – so do not hesitate to turn them down if you are offered any.

Flats with shared front entrances are not particularly desirable either, even if they do have entry phones fitted. It is too easy for a villain to con his way into an entrance hall by pressing any bell and claiming to be a delivery man. There is no efficient safeguard to ensure you will not find such a person loitering in your entrance hall when you come home.

The best kind of flat is one that is above ground floor level and has its own entrance, providing that you do not gain access to your entrance up an unlit staircase or a long, dark walkway. The very best flats have a resident caretaker who keeps a watchful eye over the block and is there to help in emergencies.

Do not be tempted to take a flat that is too high off the ground and requires the use of a lift. Lifts are like shared entrances, you never know who is in them and you run the risk of being trapped in there with an attacker. Also, lifts that are open to all and sundry seem to be readily vandalised or used as public toilets. The other unfortunate thing about lifts is that they are always breaking down, and if you are in your seventies, prone to arthritis and live on the seventeenth floor, it means that you are frequently housebound. At a price, there are some elegant blocks of flats that have a full-time porter on the front door, carpeted hallways and well-kept lifts, but they are rare.

Setting yourself high standards does not mean you need not be realistic. Do not say 'I'm young and resilient, I can put up with a vandalised block of flats because it's a cheap place to live.' You could be putting your life, or at least your health, at risk for the sake of a few pounds. Even if you escape mugging or harassment, you will not escape the depression induced by your environment.

In urban environments most of the flats on offer are in converted houses, which can be very good, or very bad. I have lived in a very good conversion and viewed some very bad ones.

The same rules apply to conversions as to purpose-built blocks: no basements and well-lit, individual entrances. If you are buying then you will have a survey done, which may point out some of the defects. Before you go to the expense of a professional survey, though, it is worth making a proper asessment yourself. You should also do this if you are renting; you are still proposing to enter into a contract with someone. Do not forget that even if you are a potential council or housing association tenant, you have the right to turn down unsuitable property or demand that certain repairs be carried out before you sign on the dotted line.

The art of viewing

When you view a flat use your eyes, ears and nose.

WHAT TO SMELL FOR Firstly notice the smell when the present occupant opens the door. It is a little difficult to describe the smell of damp to those who have not encountered it, but it is a musty odour. Your nose may be assailed by all sorts of smells, of course. If the property has been lived in for a long time with old carpets that have never been shampooed they can exude quite pungent odours.

There are other smells to beware of apart from damp. Gas, for a start. People can live for years with a small gas leak and never notice anything but always wonder why they are so tired. To a stranger the smell may be more obvious. When you go into the bathroom the smell of urine can mean that the toilet is leaking into the surrounding floorboards: an expensive business to correct. Try not to view flats when the present occupant is likely to be cooking a meal because that will effectively swamp all other smells. However, do notice whether there is a lingering odour of cooked food at other times. This may mean that the ventilation in the flat is inadequate – the kitchen may need to be fitted with an extractor fan, for example.

WHAT TO LOOK FOR Firstly, look at the layout of the flat. Some conversions that were done a long time ago would not pass today's stringent building regulations.

If the flat only has one entrance/exit (which it will because it is not on the ground floor), it should have a fire escape, or some means of escape over a balcony or roof. Seventy per cent of all fires in the home start in the kitchen, so a converted flat that has the kitchen next to the front door – the main entrance/exit – is dangerous. It means you could be trapped in the flat if fire breaks out.

Does the living room receive plenty of light? Most of your activities will be in here – sewing, reading, watching television and so on – you should not have to strain your eyes to do them.

If you can possibly afford it, opt for more than one bedroom. This gives you so much more flexibility to have people to stay, to rent out a room if you become hard up or to simply have a room to move into while you decorate your main bedroom. If you are buying a property, then always try to maximise your resale potential. Two bedroomed flats can be bought by a variety of people. A one bedroomed flat is restricted to single purchasers.

Think of flexibility again in the bathroom. A separate toilet is ideal because, if you do have people to stay, it is less of a problem if one wants to go to the toilet while someone else is having a bath. Similarly, bathrooms that can only be reached through a bedroom are not a good idea if you have guests in the bedroom which does not adjoin the bathroom.

If you are disabled in any way (even if it is only a minor disability it could become worse as you grow older) then you must view a flat from the point of view of your ease of movement. Are the doorways wide enough for a wheelchair, can you go easily from one room to another, is the floor level throughout the flat, or are there steps up and down to various rooms? Check that worktops and washbasins are the right height. Can the walls withstand the installation of special equipment such as bed-hoists or bath rails? If you are disabled you will need to take a specialist along with you to view a property to consider any problems in structural adaptation.

Still relying on your eyes, look at the window frames. Are they rotting and peeling? Are the sash cords intact? Look at the putty that secures the window frames in place. It may be old, cracked, and bits may have fallen out. Panes of glass may be cracked. All these things will have to be replaced or you will feel draughts. Look at the doors and close them. Are they hanging well, do they close properly? Are there large gaps at the top and bottom of the doors? If so there will be more draughts.

Look at taps. Are they dripping? Are they leaking from the base because the mastic has worn away? You can tell if the property has a leaky tap problem because there will usually be tell-tale stains on the washbasins. However, leaky taps are not expensive to repair, so it is not a major difficulty.

Look at the front door. From the point of view of security you do not want a door that is all glass, neither do you want a hollow plywood-type door that is easily kicked in. A solid door that has good, secure locks (preferably two – a Yale lock and a deadlock) and in which you can install a viewer, which will enable you to verify the identity of callers before opening up, is an important feature.

Look at the ceilings and the walls. Sometimes it is difficult to tell whether a ceiling is badly cracked because people cover them up with ceiling paper or tiles. Similarly with walls. You can look for damp patches though, particularly on outside walls. There will be telling changes in the colour of the wallpaper inside. Be assertive when you are viewing a property. Move sofas away from the wall and look carefully.

Look at the electrical points. If they appear new then the electrical wiring is possibly up to scratch, since no professional electrician would install new power points without checking the wiring first. Beware of anything that looks like a do-it-yourself job – crooked power points, for example. Are there enough power points? I had to install at least another four in the kitchen in my present home, to cater for all the electrical appliances. Does the flat have gas and electricity? If so, where are the meters? Do you have easy access to the stop cock that turns off the water? This is most important in an emergency, its position should be remembered and it should never be boarded up.

Look at the floors. Are they even, or do they slope in some rooms? Old conversions can be subject to settlement.

WHAT TO LISTEN FOR Are the walls solid or can you hear the neighbours clearly through them? Do the floorboards creak? Can you hear the upstairs neighbour walking across the floor? It is a good idea to view a property more than once, at different times of the day, as what may seem a peaceful haven during the day, when everyone is out, turns into a nightmare in the evening, when families come in and televisions are turned on.

All of these tips should be followed when viewing a house, with some extra points to bear in mind.

The biggest expense of any house, and its most important facet, is the roof. You will only be able to tell whether the roof is new or old. Look for moss growing on tiles, cracked tiles and damaged chimney stacks. You will need a surveyor, or a friend in the building trade, to inspect the loft and check whether all is dry and whether the timbers supporting the roof are sound.

The garden or gardens, front and back. Again be realistic about them. You will be living there on your own and, possibly, will be at work during the week. Even if you love gardening could you really cope with a total of 200 feet of garden? Remember your personal security when viewing front gardens. A long garden with plenty of tall shrubs and bushes means plenty of cover for an attacker to hide there and surprise you on your night-time walk to the front door. Have only low-level foliage in the front of the house, where only a garden gnome could hide.

Neither buy nor rent a house with a back garden that backs onto a public footpath or alleyway, or a house that has a right of way running down the side of the garden. These are security risks. Neither, if you value your privacy and security, should you buy or rent a house on the end of a road where the public pavement runs alongside your house and garden. Children are likely to play ball against your side wall and you may find yourself picking litter out of the garden which has been thrown over your wall or fence. Unfortunately, front and side gardens in urban areas are always magnets for litter louts. If the garden does not already have them, then you will be able to erect fences that are high enough to deter intruders and give you privacy of course. If, when you do, the neighbours think you are being anti-social explain or say that you have a passion for climbing roses or clematis, or make some other excuse if you wish to be polite. Be sure before you commit yourself to your chosen home that you know all about the boundaries of your property, any rights of way that exist, such as neighbours having access over your gardens, and which fences you have to maintain.

Your solicitor, during the course of making enquiries about the home you are going to buy, may not uncover a right of way because it may not be registered and the present occupant of the property may not be aware that there is a legal right. The present occupant may say 'Oh well, I let old Mrs Smith walk through my garden and down the sideway when she needs to' and regard it as no more than a neighbours' agreement. However, if this practice has persisted for more than twelve years it will have become what is known as a prescriptive right of way, and you will inherit it and not be able to do anything about it. The tell-tale signs are gaps in the fence between you and the potential neighbours, or even gates or doors.

Garages are lovely things to have, if they are attached to the house, but can be a source of grief if part of a block that is situated away from the property. You are liable to find that every time you go to use your car one of any number of people has parked in front of the garage and that neither painted notices nor threats will deter them. Also, a remote block of garages can be a personal security risk as they are often unlit. Parking one's car at night and walking through a dark garage block can be a hazard.

Staircases are things to consider carefully when buying or renting a house. Again, be realistic. If you hope that you will live for the rest of your life in this place then do not choose a house with an awkward staircase that you may not be able to negotiate when you are old. Open-plan staircases are very dangerous, as are spiral staircases. If you are going to live in a two-storey, or more, dwelling, choose one with staircases that are a reasonable width, with handrails or bannisters, well lit, with no awkward corners or sudden changes in stair depth and with well-fitting stair carpets.

Now think about the little details of your potential property, such as, if you are renting, or buying a flat, what are the service charges? A recent development in the property market has been the creation of sheltered accommodation for the elderly – both rented and private. This is an excellent idea, as it provides the elderly with independent, private accommodation but with the added security of fitted alarms linked up to a 24-hour warden service. However, some elderly people have gone to live in private developments without properly investigating all the extra costs involved. There is often a very high service charge to pay for all the administration, maintenance services – such as cleaning of communal areas and gardening – and, of course, the wardens. Many blocks of flats, for all ages, have service charges attached, so make sure you know all about them, down to the last penny, before committing yourself.

There is also something called ground rent, which is attached to leasehold flats. The person who owns the entire building, converted house or purpose-built block, sells the flats on long leases and charges the owners of the flats a ground rent. Out of this, the owner of the whole building supposedly takes some responsibility for certain external damage to the fabric of the building. When I lived in South London unscrupulous property developers were buying up the freeholds of converted houses at auctions and raising the ground rents to astronomical figures in order to force people to sell back their flats to them. Recently, there has been a movement by leasehold flat owners to band together, form a management company and buy up their own freeholds, thus ensuring that their ground rents remain low.

Active tenants' and residents' committees in your block or area are a good sign: they give you a point of contact with neighbours and usually mean that your environment is afforded some degree of protection by the efforts of these people.

Finally, we come to the bugbear of the 1980s – rubbish collection. Now that we have the practice of dustmen only collecting plastic bags that you have to place outside your residence, you have to be sure that you are capable of doing that. If you are elderly or disabled and the rubbish has to be taken down to the end of a long driveway can you cope? Some purpose-built blocks of flats fortunately have rubbish chutes on each landing, which means that you can dispose of the rubbish daily down to a large bin. If your flats do not have this communal facility, however, where do you store all the week's rubbish as it accumulates? This is a problem that is easily overlooked when viewing a property, and can be a genuine problem in the future.

RENTING A PROPERTY*

If you have never rented property before, it is worth knowing what you should expect from the contract that you are undertaking. Whether you are renting privately, from a housing association or from a council, you should have a proper tenancy agreement that gives rules of occupation, i.e. what you can or cannot do, such as keep pets, or alter the structure of the property. The agreement should also outline the landlord's obligations, such as repairs. You must also have a rent book, if you pay rent weekly, as proof of your financial transactions. You should receive receipts for all payments made which are not weekly.

Types of tenancy

There are several types of tenancy:

REGULATED TENANCIES – these can be either protected or statutory. The difference is that a protected tenant has security by virtue of his contract with the landlord; a statutory tenant has security by virtue of the protection given by the Rent Acts.

SHORTHOLD TENANCIES – a new type of regulated tenancy introduced eight years ago. These are tenancies that are for a fixed period of one to five years, after which the landlord has a guaranteed right to repossess the property. Other situations where a landlord has a guaranteed right of

*All the information in the rental section has been supplied by the Department of the Environment and the Welsh Office.

repossession are: lettings by temporarily absent owner occupiers; lettings of retirement homes – a letting that enables people to let a home to which they intend to ultimately retire; lettings by servicemen.

RESTRICTED CONTRACTS – the legal term for lettings where the landlord and tenant live in the same house. Tenants of resident landlords do not normally have long-term security of tenure, and such lettings are not subject to the fair rent system.

ASSURED TENANCIES – residential tenancies in properties that are newly built or have had at least £5000 spent on improving them in the two years before they were first let. Only landlords approved by the Secretary of State can let on assured tenancies. The landlord can let at an agreed market rent. Tenants have security of tenure during the currency of their lease.

Local authority and housing association tenants have certain rights that are laid down by government:

- The right to buy their home (after a certain period of tenancy and subject to meeting financial criteria).
- Security of tenure, subject to their landlord being able to regain possession of the property on certain defined grounds, i.e. if they do not pay their rent.
- The right of a widow, widower or resident member of their family to succeed to the tenancy on the tenant's death.
- The right to exchange their home.
- The right to take in lodgers.
- The right to sublet part of their home (as long as they do not change the use e.g. by subletting to a business concern).
- The right to repair their home.
- The right to information about their legal rights and obligations and those of their landlord.
- The right to be consulted about matters affecting their home or their tenancy.
- Certain rights about communal heating charges.

Private tenants also have certain rights:

- The right to apply to a rent tribunal to fix a fair rent.
- If they pay a service charge they have the right to obtain a summary of the costs on which their service charge is calculated and to inspect the accounts and receipts on which the summary is based.
- The right to ask a court to fix the amount they have to pay for services or works on the grounds that these have not been provided to a reasonable standard or at a reasonable cost.
- The right to ask a court to limit to what is reasonable the amount of any advance payments their lease requires them to make against a service charge.
- The right for their tenants' association to be officially recognised.
- When a tenant's right to occupy comes to an end, the tenant cannot be made to leave against his or her will, except by a court order. Eviction without a court order is a criminal offence.
- If the tenancy was granted for less than seven years, the landlord is, by law, responsible for the repair of the structure and exterior of the dwelling and for keeping in repair and proper working order any basins, sinks, baths, and other sanitary installations, and any installations for supplying gas, water, electricity, for heating water, and for space heating.
- The right to a valid notice to quit, in writing, served at least four weeks before it is due to expire, and which must also contain certain prescribed information about tenant's rights.

BUYING A HOME

Buying a property is an exercise in frustration – always. From the time you fall in love with a property to the time you move in, you can count on it being an average of three to four months. It can be much worse if you are selling as well as buying, for you are then involved in a dreaded thing called 'the chain', which only moves at the pace of the slowest, if it does not disintegrate along the way and put you back to square one.

When you find a place that is satisfactory, though, the first thing to do is to make an offer for it to the estate agent. This does not have to be the advertised price. If you genuinely think that the property is worth less than the asking price, then make a lower offer. Most vendors allow for a margin of negotiation anyway. If your offer is acceptable then you proceed by applying for a mortgage and informing your appointed solicitor or conveyancing agent of the details of the purchase, so that he or she can then make formal overtures to the vendor's solicitors.

Mortgages

Most people buy a home with the help of a mortgage via a building society, bank, insurance company, housebuilder, or local authority. However, if you are in the position of selling a larger property, which is paid for, and buying a smaller one, then you will not have to raise finance. It used to be the case that one had to find a property that one wanted to buy first and then apply for a mortgage, but some organisations will now provide a mortgage guarantee document, that is to say an assurance of the amount of money they will lend you, before you start looking for a property.

Either way, the amount of money you can borrow will be based, if you are at work, upon a multiple of your earnings – usually two-and-a-half to three times the value of your gross earnings per year. For example, if you earn £10,000 per year, then you may be able to get a mortgage of £30,000. The percentage of the purchase price that is advanced will depend upon the age of the property. Most organisations do not lend 100 per cent of the purchase price on old properties.

There is a recurrent fallacy that building societies are 'falling over themselves to give away money'. This is simply not the case and you will probably have to wait to hear if your mortgage application has been approved. They will then insist that you have a survey done before they will advance you the money.

SURVEYS There are usually two types of surveys – a valuation survey and a more in-depth one; both surveys are expensive. At first the valuation survey will be all you need. It will provide you with two sides of an A4 sheet giving you very little detail about the property except that it is or is not worth the agreed purchase price. This is where the first problems may occur. If the surveyor states that the property is most definitely not worth the agreed price and the building society will not advance you the money you need, you have three choices: abandon the property and look again, or go to another building society and hope that another surveyor will not make the same judgement, or go to your vendor's estate agent, explain the situation and hope that the vendor will drop the price. Whichever way it will have cost you the best part of £100 for the first survey, and this is not refundable.

As you can see, unless you feel that there is something suspect about the property, such as an extension which you feel may be badly constructed, or it is very old (say, 18th century) it is really not worth paying out for the more in-depth survey in the initial stages, which costs twice as much as the ordinary valuation survey.

Let us assume that the survey is fine. There will always be minor criticisms in any survey. Do not worry if your survey report undervalues the property slightly. This may have been done by the surveyor to protect the building society or bank. If the building society or bank has agreed to lend you 90 per cent of the purchase price and the surveyor says that the property is worth every bit of the asking price, then you just might go back to the society and ask for 100 per cent, based on the glowing survey report in your hand.

Conveyancing

At this stage your conveyancing agent (who may be your solicitor or a specialist dealing in conveyancing) will now make pre-contract enquiries, which means that the vendor's solicitors will answer various questions about boundaries, fences, drains, etc. A local search will be instituted, which means that the agent or solicitor will apply to the local authority for any information regarding roadworks, public footpaths, developments or anything else that might affect your property or its environs. He or she will also apply to the Land Registry for copy title deeds of the property and a potted history of the various ownerships. All this activity will take a month or more. In some parts of the country, local authorities are so behind that searches are taking two months or more. I have heard of the practice of solicitors buying local searches from the vendor's solicitors, in order to save time, but I do not know whether this is widespread.

Deposits

If the pre-contract enquiries and the local search are satisfactory then you can proceed to sign the contract and pay a deposit. This is where you may have a problem, particularly if you are a first-time buyer, because the deposit payable is usually 5 per cent of the total value of the house, sometimes even 10 per cent. That means that you have to find, for example, £2,000 to £4,000 in ready money as a deposit on a £40,000 house. The organisation lending you the money will not advance this to you, you have to find it from somewhere else – either your savings or a short-term loan.

Completing the deal

The Completion date (i.e. when you actually move in and the money for the house is handed over) is usually 28 days after the exchange of signed contracts and deposits. So you will be without your deposit money for a month at least. Of course, it will be returned to you, less all the expenses incurred in conveyancing, when you move house. It is worth mentioning here that if you are selling as well as buying, most solicitors will not allow you to use your purchaser's deposit money for your own deposit to your vendor.

If you are selling as well as buying, then the whole business is doubled up – you have to answer pre-contract enquiries from your purchaser, as well as obtaining them from your vendor, your purchaser will have a survey done and institute a local search on your property. All of this adds to the time involved in the process and certainly adds to the fees.

Fees

The fees payable for the whole process are as follows:
Arrangement fee. Some lending organisations charge a **Mortgage arrangement fee**, which can vary from a few pounds to around £50.
Valuation survey fee. Usually this is a fixed sum which, at the time of writing seems to average around £90. Average rate for a structural survey (more in-depth) seems to be around £200.
Solicitors/Conveyancing agents fee. This varies, since the introduction of registered conveyancing agents has caused solicitors to be more competitive. It is worth shopping around for the best quote possible. It will average several hundred pounds.
Stamp Duty. This is payable on all properties valued at over £30,000 and is a fixed rate of 1 per cent. Therefore the stamp duty on a house worth £70,000 is £700. Do make sure that any monies paid for fixtures and fittings are *excluded* from the registered purchase price otherwise you will pay stamp duty on them.
Land Registry fees. This varies according to the purchase price, but is an average of about £20 for a modest property.
Search fees. This varies according to the local authority involved. About the same as Land Registry fees.
Deposit. This is usually a standard ten per cent in contracts but in practice is usually agreed at five per cent.
Estate agent's commission. This is only applicable if you are

selling a property and is usually between one and two per cent of the purchase price. In real terms it can be a large sum to pay (£700–£1400 on a £70,000 sale) so think carefully when you budget for a move.

Bridging loans. If you are selling a house and buying another one, you may find yourself in a position where you have to wait for your purchaser to complete, whereas your new home is ready. You will therefore be put in the position of paying two mortgages at the same time for a short period. Unless you have enough spare cash to do this, you will have to take out a bridging loan. Interest rates on such loans vary.

Removal costs. Shop around for a reasonable estimate, or hire a van and the services of some friends and do it yourself, it is much cheaper, and worth while if you are only moving a short distance.

All that is left now is for you to move in.

ORGANISING THE MOVE

Once you have rented or bought your home, and you have fixed a date for your occupation it is time to sort out the essential services – gas, electricity, water, telephone. You will need to telephone the various local offices (local to the place where you are going to live, not where you are now) and make sure that a telephone will be laid on, the gas meter will be read, the electricity meter will be read and that all the services will be connected and functioning when you arrive on the day.

This can be difficult. If you have, for example, never been a telephone subscriber before (that is, even if you have had communal use of a telephone but it was not in your name) you will have to pay a new subscriber charge plus a connection charge. If you want to organise your energy bills to be paid monthly instead of quarterly, tell the gas and electricity boards at this stage. If you need to have your gas fire or gas cooker connected when you arrive at your new place, make sure that you tell the gas board that you need someone there on the day. It may, in fact, be better to organise it for the day after you move, because being certain that everything will run according to plan on the day of the move is almost impossible, so it is better to do without your cooker overnight and schedule this for the next morning when you know you are definitely going to be there.

If you are moving from a place other than a shared home for which you had no personal responsibility, you will need to cancel the milk and newspapers for ever, and organise new deliveries at your new address. This will necessitate a visit to the local newsagent for the papers and you will have to ask your new next door neighbour if she or he can give a note to the milkman for you or contact the local dairy yourself. You will also find it helpful to have your post redirected. This is done by going to your local post office, filling in a form and paying a small fee – the amount depends upon how long you want the post redirected for; most people find that three months is adequate.

Your change of address is important to all your friends and relatives and all those people who usually send you bills or communications – like the bank, building society, post office, insurance company etc., and you should notify them straight away.

Packing

If you are using a removal firm ask them to provide tea-chests for all the small items, and they will pack them for you. Start saving newspapers to use for wrapping china. If you are carrying out the move yourself, with the help of some friends, then do not use tea-chests, they are too heavy, start scouring your local supermarkets and off-licences for as many card-board boxes as you can lay your hands on. Select the ones that have held bottles, because they will be stapled at the bottom and are much stronger. Also look for ones that have carrying slots either side as they are much easier to manage.

Label all the boxes and make an inventory. This serves several purposes. It will: identify your belongings from those of other people that may also be in the removal van; enable you and your friends, or the removal men, to put the boxes in the right rooms (i.e. anything labelled 'crockery' in the kitchen), this saves sorting it out later on; and it will enable you to lay your hands quickly on the teapot when it is all over and you are gasping for a cuppa!

Sort out any booklets or manuals that pertain to the heating system or any other fixture that you are leaving behind. Write out a list of local phone numbers and any instructions that the next occupants of your home will find invaluable – like how to open up that funny cupboard in the second bedroom that always sticks. Ask the occupants of your next home if they would please do the same thing.

Start running down the food in your freezer and fridge, so that they can be switched off and cleaned a couple of days before you move. Clear out your food cupboard and throw away everything that will not travel well, such as leaky, crushable or carbonated goods. Make a list of what essential food you will need for the first day in your new home and go shopping the day before you move.

Clear out all your possessions and be ruthless. Now is the time to take rubbish to the dump, to give things away to charity shops and jumble sales. There is no point in taking all your useless rubbish with you. Also clear up the garden. You are not supposed to leave rubbish behind for the next occupants to cope with, although you can leave it bagged up outside the door for the dustmen to take later. If you are leaving the area do not forget to pick up any clothes that are at the cleaners, or shoes, clocks, or other items that are away being mended. You will also need to withdraw sufficient cash from the bank to pay for the removal. It is common practice to tip the people who have done the removal work so you may want to withdraw enough for this too.

On the day of the removal, board any pets with friends for the day, it is too upsetting for them and, anyway, dogs and cats might be under your feet. Pack everything except some cleaning materials and the vacuum cleaner so that you can clean all the corners and places where hidden dirt is revealed when the furniture is removed.

You may want to make the nice gesture, which was made to me when I first moved into a flat and I have repeated myself whenever I have moved, of leaving a plant or a box of chocolates and a note wishing the next occupants a happy life in your former home.

3·YOUR HOME IS YOUR CASTLE

Whether you have just moved into a new home or have been living in the same place for years the main thing is that you are alone and you must make your home your pride, your joy, your sanctuary. That is the first step towards making your life alone happy and healthy. The aim of this chapter is to provide help in making your home secure, comfortable, economical and beautiful whether you are with friends or alone.

SECURITY IS THE FIRST PRIORITY

A secure home can be achieved without any great expense and with a little organisation. It will banish any anxieties that you may have about being alone at night or coming home to an empty house. Your well-being is the most important thing and you start by creating some peace of mind.

Personal safety

- If you lose your keys, or if someone steals your keys, or if you move into a new home and you do not know who may have spare keys change all the locks immediately.
- Never announce to a group of strangers or in a crowded public place that you live alone. Someone could follow you home after overhearing your conversation.
- Close all windows and lock them when you go out. The same goes for doors.
- Never open the front door to a caller unless you know the person. If anyone claims to be from the Gas Board, Electricity Board, council, or any such body, keep the chain on the door and tell them that you only admit such people by

appointment. You have that right. Many people have been tricked by villains with false identity cards. Do you know what a Gas Board ID should look like? The essential services have no statutory right of entry unless there is an emergency. They can quite easily send you a postcard telling you when a meter inspector will call. Do not even admit someone claiming to be a policeman or woman. Again, do you know all the correct details of a uniform and identity card? The police have no right of entry without a warrant and will certainly understand if you explain politely that you are reluctant to let them in.

- Never tell local shopkeepers that you are going on holiday, or announce the fact in a public place. Again, you do not know who may be listening.
- Never announce to the world that you have gone away by forgetting to cancel the milk and newspapers. Ask a neighbour to collect your post, water your plants (dead plants or plants that are regularly on windowsills suddenly removed are tell-tale signs) and perhaps to draw your curtains every night. Use an automatic time switch on your lighting.
- Phone the police if you see anyone whom you regard as suspicious loitering close by or if you suspect a potential intruder is lurking nearby.
- When you answer the phone, just say 'hello' and do not give your name and number. Better still, if you live alone, have an ex-directory number.

Property Risks

- Does the front garden provide good cover for a burglar to work on your windows unseen from the road?
- Is your house detached and secluded? This is a magnet to burglars and you need to take all the precautions you can to control access.
- Is your back garden so secluded that it is not overlooked by any other property and thus provides another unseen point of entry for a burglar?

- Do you have a flat roof at the rear of the house that could provide easy access to upstairs windows?
- Do you have solid iron downpipes that could be climbed?
- Do you have an enclosed unlit porch that would give a housebreaker some cover while working on the front door lock?
- Do you have either or both double-glazed windows and window locks? They make windows much more difficult to break into.
- Do you have more than one lock on the front door, bolts, a safety chain, a view-hole, and/or an entryphone? Despite everything, a lot of burglaries are still carried out via the front door. An ordinary lock can easily be bypassed with a strip of plastic.
- Does your house have a side access to the back of the building?
- Does your garden back onto an alley or road?
- Does your flat have a balcony or roof garden?
- Does your flat, conservatory, or utility room have a sky-light to the roof?
- Do you leave a ladder in the greenhouse or garden shed or leaning against the kitchen wall?
- Do you have evidence of an alarm system on the outside wall of the house? Even an unwired alarm box is often sufficient to deter a burglar.
- Do you have exterior lights on the house?
- Are all your expensive goods easily seen from windows?
- Are you part of a Neighbourhood Watch scheme and if so do you display stickers attesting to the fact?
- Do you have a dog? Still the greatest burglar deterrent known to man.
- Do you leave spare keys in hiding places outside the house? Leave a spare key with a trustworthy neighbour. Do not leave keys hanging in obvious places inside the house. If a burglar breaks in through a window, he will want to open the door so that he can carry the television out to his vehicle. If the door has good locks on it, he will not be able to open the door without keys.

- Do you have a flimsy, glass-panelled back door?

How vulnerable is your property in the light of these points?

Make your windows as difficult to break in to as possible. The opportunist housebreaker will not shirk from breaking a window, of course, but the more levels of protection you create, the more time it will take him – which is a risk he may not wish to take. Secondary double glazing, by which means additional window frames are fixed into fitments inside your existing windows, is not prohibitively expensive. Window locks are fairly cheap and absolutely essential. It is a good idea to fill your window sills with ornaments and plants, which will prevent any intruder from making a noiseless entry.

If your house is detached and secluded, then you must think about spending quite a bit of money on boundary protection – high walls and fences with added obstructions on top, such as trellis or privet. You may not, however, top your wall with broken glass or barbed wire without the consent of your local authority. Remember that all fences, walls and gates should be sheer, not ornamented. In other words, there should be no footholds for an agile intruder. Decorative projecting bricks, alcoves, wrought iron gates, and so on, are a security risk.

Another deterrent around a house is gravel. It makes it impossible for anyone to creep around your house without making a noise. Gravel is particularly useful to lay over a side access. The deeper it is, the more it scrunches.

Whether or not you have a dog, display a sign on the front gate that says 'Beware of the dog'. It has the same effect as the fake burglar alarm box – the intruder will think twice and move on to another house that does not present any problems.

The outside of any house or flat should be well lit at night. Floodlights are not necessary, although if you have a large garden you may consider strategic lighting within the grounds, but the back and front door should have lights that come on automatically at dusk and stay on until dawn. Enclosed porches should always be well lit at night.

Automatic time switches attached to your lighting system are easy to fit and a marvellous idea for those who live alone. These devices can be set by you to switch lights on and off for determined periods while you are away from home. This means that while you are out for the evening, anyone who may be watching the house will be unsure as to whether you are at home or not, because various lights will go on and off at different times. If you do not buy one of these make sure that you always leave some lights switched on inside the house – even if you are going out at eight o'clock in the morning and will not be back until midnight. A few pence on the electricity bill is nothing compared with your security.

Replace all metal drainpipes with plastic ones (which are far too flimsy for anyone to scale), remove any trees near the house that would assist ascent to the first floor and absolutely never leave ladders outside the house, front or back, always *lock* them away.

The easiest place for a burglar to gain access to a house is through patio doors. Make sure that yours are fitted with all possible locks and are constructed of unbreakable glass. If you have inherited patio doors from the previous owner and it would be too expensive to replace them, you might consider having a sliding grille fitted behind the doors, which can be pulled across and locked when you are out. There are, of course, many alarm systems that you could fit to a home and prices range enormously. It is best to take advice from a good security expert.

If you are elderly, you may be eligible for financial assistance to buy security equipment. If you are a tenant, your landlord should certainly be liable for ensuring that all windows, frames and doors are in good condition.

PERSONAL SAFETY INSIDE THE HOME

The biggest hazard inside the home is fire. Earlier in the book I spoke about making sure you have adequate escape routes in the event of fire, now we will talk about fire prevention. Good internal doors, which should be kept closed as much as possible, can halt a fire by up to twenty minutes, allowing you time to escape. Make sure all doors fit well and have draught excluders.

The kitchen is the prime source of home fires but there are some guidelines to avoiding disaster:

- Never leave pans that are cooking, particularly chip pans or frying pans. Turn them off if you have to answer the door or the phone.
- Do not hang oven gloves or teatowels over cookers.
- Remove polystyrene tiles from a kitchen ceiling, they burst into flames and melt, dropping red hot liquid onto anything that is below, and polystyrene also exudes toxic gases.
- Do not put aerosol containers anywhere near a cooker.
- Do not have portable heaters in the kitchen.
- Make sure that there is always adequate ventilation in a kitchen, when cooking, to prevent heat from an oven building up in a confined space.
- Keep a proper fire blanket in the kitchen to be used for smothering fat fires. Do not use a fire extinguisher or water on fat fires.

Heating is another danger area but, likewise, you can take preventative steps:

- Open fires should always have a fireguard.
- Open fires should always have the chimney regularly swept, otherwise the build up of soot can start a chimney fire.
- Never hang clothes on a dryer in front of a fire or an open heater. One spark and the whole of your week's washing could start a conflagration.
- Never stand over an open fire as Victorian fathers used to do. A spark can just as easily set light to your clothes as it can to a dryer full of washing.

- Make sure that you do not leave newspapers or magazines on top of open heaters.
- Always put out an open fire before going to bed.
- Do not put fluffy rugs in front of open fires, where they are in the direct line of sparks.
- Do not try to draw up an open fire with a sheet of newspaper. Nine times out of ten it will catch fire in your hands.
- Do not throw rubbish onto an open fire in the living room. Many packaging materials contain highly flammable substances that could make a fire suddenly flare up. Also, you may throw on the fire something that gives off toxic fumes.
- Make sure that any portable heaters are stable (and, particularly in the case of bottled gas or paraffin, that you have adequate ventilation in the room).
- Do not buy foam-filled furniture if you can avoid it, as it can give off lethal fumes when it ignites. Modern furniture should be fire-proof but your budget may dictate that you buy second-hand. Be very careful when choosing. Wooden-framed furniture is best, then at least you can change the cushions for less flammable material.

If you suspect a gas leak at any time, do not strike a match or even turn on the electric light, as that can produce a minute spark that can cause an explosion. Ensure that all your gas appliances are regularly serviced.

Safety with electricity means never operating anything that has a worn or damaged flex; never trying to run an appliance from a light socket; never trying to run several appliances via an adaptor plugged into one socket; and ensuring that all plugs are wired properly. If you have a power cut, try to switch everything off, except perhaps a light, in case the power comes back on while you are asleep or out.

Beware of cigarettes, cigars and pipes, particularly near furniture and never smoke in bed. Never leave a smoking substance in an ashtray and walk away from it. Never empty ashes into cane or rush wastepaper baskets.

The Fire Service recommends that people seriously consider installing smoke detectors in their homes, following a spate of fire deaths in 1987. These are suitable for every room except the kitchen. They are easy to install, as most are battery operated. They are also reasonably priced. They do, however, need to be tested at monthly intervals to ensure that the batteries are still active. Fire extinguishers may seem a good idea, but there are so many types to be used for so many different sorts of fires that I would be nervous of escalating a fire, rather than killing it, by using the wrong type of extinguisher. It is worth remembering that water can be used to douse any kind of fire except a fat fire or a fire involving electrical equipment.

AVOIDING ACCIDENTS IN THE HOME

The home is a hazardous place, and not just if you are elderly, in fact more accidents happen to the young, who tend to rush about more and trip over things or fall down staircases.

Preventative action is as viable here as for fire hazards. Do not forget that you live alone and there may not be anyone there to pick you up or ring for the doctor if you break a leg or a hip.

If you are a person who is classified as being 'at risk', that is elderly, frail or disabled in some way, then you should seriously consider either living in a sheltered housing complex where you have the safety net of alarms in every room rigged to a 24-hour warden service, or subscribing to a medical alert system. The latter is either a private network, or one set up by the local authority in your area which operates an alarm system at a central control point. Alarms can either be rigged up in every room in your house, or you can wear an alarm unit on your person, to activate in times of need. The alarm will trigger in a central control point and the people there will either ring a neighbour to ask them to go and see what the problem is, or immediately ring the emergency services. If you want to find out what is available in your area, ask the social services department or your local health visitor.

Whether you are young or old, you should always leave a key with a neighbour whom you trust and who is at home quite often, maybe someone who is retired, or who is at home with children, in case there is an emergency while you are out. The real value of a key deposited with a neighbour comes when you are ill or incapacitated and can only call for help or reach the phone, but not reach the front door.

Further to this point, always have a telephone on every floor of your house. Someone of my acquaintance once broke her ankle by falling over in the bathroom and while she could have dragged herself quite easily along the floor to a telephone in the bedroom if she had had one, as it was it took her the best part of an agonising hour to struggle down the stairs to the phone in the living room.

Accident blackspots

There are several accident black spots in the home.

FLOORS Wherever there is water or liquid, there is the danger of it ending up on the floor and causing you to slip. The best thing to do is to put down absorbent floor covering in those rooms. Do not, whatever you do, lay down loose rugs, they are guaranteed to trip you up. A washable fitted carpet is best in the bathroom and well-fitting washable carpet tiles, with a backing material that prevents it from creeping, in the kitchen. That is what I have in my kitchen and I find that it is very simple to lift and scrub the tiles that take the most punishment, like the ones by the cooker. The value of absorbent flooring is that anything dropped, such as cooking oil (highly dangerous underfoot) immediately disappears instead of laying there waiting to send you sliding.

KITCHENS Arrange your kitchen, if necessary, so that the sink is very close to the cooker. Many scalding accidents occur when people move from the cooker to the sink to drain off boiling hot vegetables and either trip or drop the pan.

Never leave objects on the floor of the kitchen, such as shoes or dustpans, that may trip you up as you back away from the sink or cooker.

Do not pile up plates or saucepans higgeldy-piggeldy on a high shelf, where they can so easily fall on top of you when you reach up for something. You should not have shelving too high anyway. Discs are easily slipped by an over-stretching movement.

BATHROOMS In the bathroom, put a non-slip bathmat in the bottom of the bath. Slipping and injuring yourself in the bath is not only painful but life-threatening. If you knock yourself out you could slip under the water and drown.

Do not put shelves or bathroom cabinets immediately above the washbasin. A friend of mine concussed himself by bending over to splash his face in the basin and cracking his head on a cabinet as he straightened up.

Never take electrical appliances into the bathroom. It is simply not safe to have radios on the side of the bath, or electrical heaters plugged in to the bathroom in winter, or to sit in the bath while shaving with an electric razor. The combination of water and electricity means instant death – not a mild shock – death. In fact power points are illegal in bathrooms, all except small razor sockets. If you do not have a heated bathroom then invest in a high wall-mounted heater, which has to be the type approved for bathroom use, and should be connected through the wall to a power source outside the room. Otherwise you could invest in a thermal light bulb – they throw out a lot of heat. A free-standing oil or water filled radiator is all right too, providing, again, the power source is outside the bathroom. Any major appliance in the bathroom, such as a washing machine or tumble drier, should always have a properly routed power source outside the bathroom itself. In other words, the cable should be taken through a hole in the wall to the hallway or bedroom. Never trail a cable through the bathroom door.

Do not sit in the hottest bath that you can stand, because this can make you feel faint and you could pass out when you stand up. Similarly, do not have a hot bath after a heavy meal or after drinking alcohol – the same thing could happen.

STAIRS In the previous chapter I urged you to pick a property where the stairs were of adequate width (this means wide enough for your body but preferably wide enough for two people to pass), well-lit, no awkward corners, no sudden changes in stair depth, with good handrails or bannisters. Make sure that stair carpets are secure and there are no loose treads or worn pieces.

Treat stairs with respect if you want to avoid accidents. Do not put piles of books or magazines up the sides of the stairs. Do not attempt to carry something up or down the stairs that is heavy, awkward, or restricts your vision, so that you cannot see where you are placing your feet. Do not leave objects on the stairs. It is so easy to do, but if you leave a tin of polish and the duster on the stairs say, while you go up and then have to dash down to answer the front door bell, you can easily slip on them.

Do not wear slippers without any backs in them. You cannot traverse staircases safely in anything other than well-fitting slippers. Nor are glamorous stiletto shoes safe until you are at the bottom of the stairs; do not attempt to come down wearing them as the danger is very real – Winston Churchill's mother lost a leg that way.

Around the house generally, do not allow electrical flexes to trail over the floor. Make sure that tall, free-standing furniture, like bookcases, is stable. Do not stand on chairs to reach something at ceiling level. Bend down at the knees to pick up a bulky object, thus avoiding back strain. If you are an 'at risk' person, and not very stable on your feet, or walk with an aid, do not have open fires in the house – you could fall on them and be badly burned. The social services department should be able to fit even ordinary radiators with some sort of guard, so that if you should fall against them and be unable to move, you are not pinned against something that is uncomfortably or dangerously hot.

GARDENS In the garden, never leave tools laying on the ground, particularly rakes or shears that you can step on and impale yourself. Make sure that all sharp implements, such as scythes, have covers, and hang all your tools up, never just throw them into a shed in a muddle. Plunging your hand into a pile of assorted implements can be hazardous. Do not keep flammable substances, such as bottled gas or paraffin, in a greenhouse, where they are likely to become overheated. Be careful with toxic substances and always follow the directions on the bottles with great care.

RUBBISH DISPOSAL When putting out rubbish, make sure that you wrap broken glass or china in several layers of newspaper to prevent you and the dustmen from being cut. (Dustmen have started sueing householders for any negligence that causes them injury.) Be very careful of old fluorescent light tubes, which can explode if dropped, and never puncture old aerosol cans or throw them on a fire.

MAKING YOURSELF COMFORTABLE

Comfort, to me, means warmth, and whenever I change homes the first thing I do is make it as warm as possible. This often means great economy too, for eliminating draughts and adding insulation will save pounds on energy bills.

Windows

If you do not have double glazing, then think about putting it in, at least for some of your windows.

Secondary double glazing is quite reasonable in price and is fairly easily fitted. Armed with a saw and a screwdriver I have fitted my own secondary units and, now, some companies are producing panes that are made of high-resilience plastics, which are much lighter to handle and are much warmer to the touch than glass. Secondary double-glazing involves the fitting of a wooden or plastic frame a few inches inside your existing window and slotting in sliding panes of glass or non-glass. Large DIY centres stock the complete kits, which will fit any standard-sized window. Of course, if you can afford full double-glazing then you have no problems, and it does actually add value to a property, providing it is in a style sympathetic to the house itself.

If you are on a really stringent budget, there are many very cheap ways of making your windows less energy-draining in the winter. Firstly, plug all the draughts with strips of foam draught excluder, but make sure that you can still open the windows properly. You can then make your own form of secondary double glazing by buying some heavy-duty clear plastic sheeting and stretching this across the inside of the window frame. You must be able to remove it quickly in case of fire, or some other emergency, so attach it to the window surround with double-sided tape, which can be easily ripped away or frequently replaced if you want to open up all the windows for a weekly blast of fresh air through the home. If you have the sort of windows that are multi-paned, you can stretch cling-film across each pane. But stretch it very tight like a drum, or it will not have the effect of keeping out the cold. Have heavy curtains at all the windows to cut out draughts and keep in the warmth, or add thermal linings to your existing curtains.

Doors

It is relatively easy to fit metal, plastic, or foam strips around the sides of the doors to exclude draughts. The metal strips with a thick brush on the bottom are best for the bottom of the door, as they will not ruin your carpets. Do this to all your doors, not just the exterior ones, and treat any panes of glass in doors as though they were windows and give them some sort of double glazing.

The external doors, of course, admit the greatest number of draughts, so apart from fitting excluders, it is also worth hanging a heavy curtain over the inside of the front and back doors. The curtain must be capable of being drawn across and back – no matter how bad the winter, you will be answering the door occasionally! Do not forget letter boxes, they can be fitted with brush-type excluders too, or you can fit a box on the back.

Radiators

Radiators are rarely used to their greatest effect. Shelves over the top of radiators push warm air down into a room. Fixing aluminium foil behind radiators, dull side against the wall, helps to reflect heat outwards, instead of letting it be absorbed by the wall.

Insulation

With all the draughts that bring cold air in blocked off you now need to insulate in order to keep the warmth in.

LOFTS As much as 25 per cent of home heat is lost through an uninsulated roof. In most cases, providing the timbers in your roof are sound and you can walk about up there, you can easily insulate the loft yourself. There are two types of material you can buy in any DIY store – insulating mats, which come in rolls, and loose granular material, which comes in sacks. The mats are unrolled and laid between the joists, while the granular insulation is just poured onto the boards. Loft insulation should be at least 4 inches (100 mm) thick in order to be effective. So if you are insulating with granules, then take a ruler up there with you to measure the depth as you go along. Follow all instructions on the packages as insulating material can be toxic.

If you have a house with an uninsulated flat roof, it can be an expensive operation to insulate, as the roofing material needs to be stripped off and several layers of insulation put underneath before re-felting. Putting a layer of polystyrene, either in tile or roll form, onto the ceiling of a room under a flat roof can help, but remember, not if this room is a kitchen.

WATER TANKS AND PIPES Insulating water tanks is the next job and this can be done with special padded material, secured in place by wire, or with special ready-made padded jackets, or, if you have a standard-sized water tank, with special pre-cut packs of sheet insulation that are placed around the tank and secured with tape or wire.

Water pipes in the loft and in any unheated room, such as a utility room, should be lagged with strips of insulating material wrapped around and around, or with special pre-formed insulation that fits neatly around a pipe.

FLOORS It is estimated that 15 per cent of home heat is lost through timber floors. You may live in a modern house where the style of bare floorboards is acceptable, but nothing beats good carpeting as insulation. In an old house, it may be that gaps in the skirting boards are the chief causes of heat loss and/or draughts, in which case a quick brandishing of wood filler around the home will solve that problem. You can, if you like, take up the floor boards and fill underneath with the same granular insulation material used in the loft, but that is a rather difficult job – not one to attempt without help.

WALLS The only thing left if your house or flat is still not as warm as you would like is wall insulation. Cavity walls can be filled by a contractor who will advise you on the best type of material for your type of property. There has been some bad press in recent years about the use of foam in cavity wall insulation and its possible side-effects on people's health. Make sure you talk to several reputable contractors before making the final decision.

Solid walls can only really be insulated by applying a material to the exterior of the walls (rendering, false York-stone, pebbledash, etc.) to make the walls thicker, or by panelling the inside of the walls. Interior panels can either be of fairly basic wood that will be papered over, or fancy panelling, such as oak, that will be left bare and make a modest property look like a stately home. Whatever panelling you use, and the latter is going to be more expensive, a layer of insulating material should be placed between the panels and the solid wall.

An excellent booklet called *Making the Most of Your Heating* is published by the Energy Efficiency Office, as well as other information that will help you to do a lot of insulating work yourself. The Office can also give information on grants that are available to certain people who, at present, have no insulation in their home at all. The elderly and disabled can obtain quite substantial financial help from several sources. All the EEO booklets are available from your local Electricity Board Showroom.

THE ART OF GRACIOUS LIVING

It may be difficult, but keeping your home clear of clutter is the first step. When I first set up home on my own I had so many bits of ill-assorted furniture that various friends and relatives had given me, that it was difficult to ever imagine having a beautiful home. What with piles of ironing (this was during my disorganised period), mountains of books (I refuse to be parted from them), and various bric-a-brac, my flat always looked like a junkyard.

Hoarding things is the main problem. Regularly throw out old magazines: give them to your dentist or the local paper-collection. Weed out some of your books occasionally and give them to jumble sales or charity shops. In my first flat I had a very large cupboard that was always filled with things I could never find a use for, or I had forgotten about. When one day I tidied up and cleared out this cupboard, I realised that I had ignored everything in it for over a year. I filled up cardboard boxes with its contents and took them down to the local charity shop. For a while I adopted the practice of putting things away in cupboards until I was in a mood to be ruthless, but now I have advanced to instant ruthlessness.

Ridding yourself of clutter does not just mean organising things into tidy piles, it means either being properly rid of them or putting them in or on something – like shelves. Shelves are cheap to buy and easy to erect. Once all your books and ornaments are on shelves there will be much more floor space.

If you do not have an airing cupboard or somewhere useful to hide all the ironing while you are steeling yourself to do it, then buy an ottoman. I have several such boxes. I have one in the bathroom for dirty washing, which doubles as a seat; I have one in my bedroom for ironing and one in the other bedroom that holds all my sewing materials. I also have one in the corner of the living room that holds all the dog's toys and blankets. The marvellous thing about basic cheap ottomans is that you can paint them any colour to match the prevailing decor of the room and you can cover the lid with padded material, or even carpet, to make a seat.

Furniture

If you cannot afford or do not want new furniture, then start to attack the soft furnishings. That is the cheapest way of giving some co-ordination and colour to your home. Nice curtains and matching scatter cushions do wonders for a jaded living room. An old sofa can be covered with a throw-over piece of material, you need not go the expense of re-upholstery or even stretch or loose covers.

An old dining table is transformed by a beautiful tablecloth and old dining chairs can be perked up by attaching seat cushions that match the colour of the tablecloth. You can totally rejuvenate a dining table and chairs bought from a junk shop by painting them with gloss paint and buying a matching or contrasting tablecloth and seat cushions for the chairs. The whole exercise is very cheap.

Plants

I could not personally live without plants. They create such a wonderful display, add life and colour to a room, and it is a joy to nurture them. But then I love growing houseplants. If you would rather not grow your own, or you do not have the time to look after them, you could do worse than invest in artificial plants, which are quite stunningly realistic nowadays. I have one, a huge 'weeping fig', which dominates a very dark corner of one room and looks most impressive. It was expensive but will last a lifetime and only needs the occasional sponging down. There are some very modestly priced artificial plants to be had. Or dried flowers are another trouble-free splash of nature in a room.

Decorating

The aim is for bright and cheerful surroundings. Everything you do when you live alone should be part of a plan to ward off depression. There is nothing more depressing than sitting and watching the paper peel off the walls. It is cheap to decorate and good therapy too. If you are elderly or disabled, your local Council of Voluntary Service should be able to provide you with willing volunteers to come and decorate for you. Or you could do what my elderly neighbour does: everytime she feels like decorating she pays a neighbour's student son to come in and do it for her.

There is no point in painting over dirt, though. Keeping your home clean will imbue you with a sense of virtue and pride in it, which will reflect positively on your own mood. It is difficult when you are at work all week, to find the time and it is not much fun spending your only free time cleaning. If you have a reasonable income, though, why not pay someone to do it? If you are elderly or disabled avail yourself of the home help service. You are entitled to some help, it is not a matter into which pride should enter.

If you are a student or a young penurious worker try this ruse a fellow student of mine developed. When we were at college he used to invite people to 'cleaning parties' once a month. Everyone had to bring a cloth, bucket and duster and he guaranteed to provide a few large bottles of cheap wine and a cheap and cheerful meal like a curry or a paella. They were great fun. I held a painting party once, along the same lines. I had a huge living room that needed repainting and so I invited a few friends along, asked them to bring a paintbrush each and I supplied the food and drink. We, did the room in one day.

NOW PUT YOUR FEET UP AND INDULGE YOURSELF

Comfort also means indulgence. When you have cleaned, polished, decorated, made yourself secure, safe and warm, you are entitled to treat yourself. If you want to spend your Sundays curled up on the sofa, watching television, and having a few drinks, why not? You do not have to worry about anyone else.

Because you live alone, you can devote yourself to making your life easier whenever possible. You cannot spend all your time cooking and cleaning and working. If you can afford it, buy some labour-saving devices, like a washing machine. Laundrettes are fast disappearing anyway, and you cannot spend your time washing everything by hand. I bought my first washing machine cheaply through an advertisement in the local paper. The machine gave good service for just over a year and then I bought my next one on interest-free credit.

I could not live without a steam iron, or an electric kettle. These are the sort of things you might suggest that people give you for your birthday, Christmas or other religious celebration. I got my food processor that way, and my slo-cooker, and my clock/alarm radio.

Televisions, radios and stereo systems bring untold pleasure to countless numbers of people who live alone. I have to confess that I saved up for a portable television before I saved up for a washing machine, but then my priorities may have been different if I had not had a laundrette opposite the front door. Of course, buying a television means you will need a television licence as well. Buying weekly television licence stamps can ease the burden somewhat and certain elderly or disabled people are able to receive help from the local authority with the cost of a licence.

No matter how small the treat, or labour saving device you are able to afford, though, it is the principle that is important.

You must always create things to look forward to, to enjoy and you must always reward yourself each week. It may just be with a weekly magazine and a cream cake, but you are giving yourself a pat on the back. If you love yourself, you will love your own company the more. Neglect yourself and self-doubt begins to creep in and that swiftly turns to depression.

4·MANAGING MONEY

When you live alone, money assumes a greater importance than if you share your life with someone. Why? You have no family to feed and clothe, you should have less of a problem. But the old saying 'a problem shared is a problem halved' is very true. Two people can cope with money worries better than one. You only have yourself to fall back on, unless, of course, you count a friendly bank manager who might lend you some money, or a friend or relative who might do the same. But borrowing money that you are going to have difficulty paying back only adds to your anxieties. So try to avoid it.

The way to manage money is firstly to assess what you have coming in and what you have to pay out. Budgeting is an instant turn-off to many people. Organising your financial well-being, however, will prove more relaxing in the long run. To be fair to yourself you should be certain that you are bringing in as much money as you should.

IS ENOUGH MONEY COMING IN?

Many people never check that their tax code is correct, and never investigate the allowances, grants or benefits that they may be entitled to. As a result they may always be hard up without needing to be.

At the time of writing, (Spring 1989), personal tax and benefits are currently as follows:

Tax

The personal allowances and reliefs (income that you are allowed to earn without being taxed) that pertain to a single person are as follows:

1989/90 Single person under the age of 65 £2785
Widow's bereavement allowance (additional to the single person's allowance for two years after husband's death. Widowers do not obtain this benefit, merely a tax repayment if their wife was working up until her death) £1590
Single person over the age of 65 (this is instead of the younger single allowance, not in addition) £3400
Single person over the age of 75 £3540
Blind person's allowance (in addition to any of the above) £540

For the purposes of tax assessment there are various types of income. When you fill in a tax return you will have to declare all sources of income and the Inland Revenue will ignore them or deduct tax as necessary.

Income where tax has been deducted at source and on which you will therefore not be required to pay further tax is as follows:

- Building society, bank and Giro deposit accounts;
- Interest from shares in British companies;
- Income from annuities (more about these later);
- Interest on Local Authority loans;
- Interest on Government Gilt Edged Securities.

Income which *should* have tax deducted at source:

- Earnings from full-time, part-time or casual employment;
- Pensions from previous employments or from deceased spouse's employer.

State on your tax return income from which tax has not been deducted at source and will therefore be assessed for tax by the Inland Revenue if it forms part of a more substantial income:

- Industrial death benefit;
- Unemployment and supplementary benefits. (This is not taxable if you are a man aged over 65, a woman aged over

60, or a man aged 60 or over who is entitled to the long-term scale rate of supplementary benefit);
- National Insurance retirement pension;
- Widows pension, widows allowance.

Private income from which income tax has not been deducted and which will therefore be assessed by the Inland Revenue:

- Business profits from self-employment or partnership. (This includes things like catalogue agencies and football pools collection.)
- Rental income from renting out property;
- Interest from bank investment accounts;
- Interest on ordinary National Savings Accounts;
- Income from abroad (shares, pensions, etc.);
- Income from trusts;
- Repayments of insurance policies within the first four years of the policy's life;
- Interest from Government Securities purchased through the Post Office;
- Interest from loans to other people.

Income that is exempt from tax:

- Education grants and awards;
- Winnings from betting, football pools, and premium bonds;
- Strike pay;
- Social security benefits as follows: Attendance Allowance, Income Support, Housing Benefit, Industrial Injuries Disablement Benefit, Invalidity Benefit, Mobility Allowance, Miscellaneous Disease Benefit, Severe Disablement Allowance, Sickness Benefit, Social Fund Payments, Government Training Allowance, War Pensions;
- Redundancy pay;
- Home Improvement Grants (not loans);
- Compensation for loss of office/position up to £30,000;

- Interest and bonuses on National Savings Certificates and the SAYE scheme. Interest from Index-linked Savings Certificates;
- Interest on delayed tax repayments;
- Alimony/maintenance payments received. The rules cover not only cash payments but also the settlement of household bills.

After your allowances have been deducted you pay the basic rate of tax (25 per cent) on any income up to £11,400 for people over 65, and £20,700 for people under 65.

There are certain expenses that you can offset against tax, which you should put down on your tax form.

- Interest on certain loans. The qualifying limit for house purchase loans and for loans to persons aged 65 and over to purchase life annuities secured on their main residence is £30,000. In the 1988 Budget this was changed to apply to the residence only and not to the individual. So the single person now receives the same tax relief on a £30,000 mortgage as a couple. The 1988 Budget also abolished tax relief on home improvement loans (grants are still tax free).
- Charitable covenants. Covenanted donations to charities for a term of more than three years can be offset against tax if you are someone who pays the higher rate of tax.

  Employees who donate up to £480 to charity through their pay at work will receive tax relief.
- Expenses against earnings. Any expenses incurred as part of a job, or as a self-employed person, providing the necessary receipts are kept.
- Fees or subscriptions to necessary professional organisations e.g. the BMA if you are a doctor, can be offset.

After April 1989 the tax relief on life assurance premiums was reduced to 12.5 per cent.

Divorced people paying alimony will receive tax relief only on an amount equal to the difference between the married man's allowance and the single person's allowance. This relief will not increase if payments are made to more than one ex-spouse. Relief will not be due for any payments made direct to children of the marriage or any previous marriage.

There are many useful leaflets you can obtain from the Inland Revenue and from the various organisations listed at the back of the book, that will help you if you find your tax situation confusing. If you are elderly or widowed, organisations like Age Concern and CRUSE will actually help you with the practical details and, if not in either of these categories, you could do no better than go to your nearest Citizens' Advice Bureau for some help.

Social Security benefits

The Social Security system is not a charity. Many truly deserving individuals do not realise what they are entitled to, or are too misguidedly proud to claim what is actually their money. You, or your parents, have paid into the system for many years, so you are entitled to claim when you are in need. All figures quoted below are for weekly payments.

- Attendance Allowance. This is payable to infirm or disabled people, ostensibly so that they can pay someone to come in and look after their needs. At the moment the rates are £22.00 for those who may need partial assistance and £32.95 for those who need full-time assistance.
- Housing Benefit. The maximum housing benefit you can receive is 100 per cent of your eligible rent and 80 per cent of your eligible rates. This is now administered by your local authority. When you claim Income Support, the DHSS will also give you a Housing Benefit claim form, which they will then pass on to the council.
- Income Support. This is a social security benefit to help people who do not have enough money to live on. You may be eligible for it even if you have savings of up to £6000, you own your own home, or you have never paid National Insurance contributions. Income Support is not available

to anyone who works for more than 24 hours a week. If you qualify for Income Support then you may also receive, in addition to the allowances listed below, free NHS prescriptions, free dental treatment, help with the cost of travelling to hospital for NHS treatment and vouchers to help with the cost of glasses. Personal allowances, premiums and payments to cover certain housing costs together make up the benefit payment. This is broken up as follows:

Personal allowances for single people

	£
Aged 16–17	19.40
Aged 18–24	26.05
Aged 25 or over	33.40

In addition to this certain premiums are paid

Pensioner	10.65
Higher pensioner (over 80)	13.05
Disabled person	13.05
Severely disabled person (in receipt of Attendance Allowance)	24.75

- Hostels and board and lodging accommodation. The maximum amount for board and lodging accommodation and meals is £55. The maximum amount for hostel acccommodation and meals is £70. On top of that you can claim for certain personal expenses. Certain groups can have an addition of £17.50.
- Industrial Injuries Disablement Benefit.

Disablement	Over 18	Under 18
	£	£
100 per cent	67.20	41.15
then the amounts are graded down to		
20 per cent	13.44	8.23

Pensions for pneumoconiosis and byssinosis assessment (at any age)

	£
1 to 10 per cent	6.72
11 to 19 per cent	13.44

Constant attendance allowance under the Industrial
Injuries Disablement Benefit scheme.

	£
Part-time rate	13.45
Normal maximum rate	26.90
Intermediate rate	40.35
Exceptional rate	53.80

Exceptionally severe disablement allowance (under IID)

	£
One rate	26.90

Unemployability supplement (under IID)

	£
Basic rate	41.15

There are additions for early incapacity:

	£
Higher rate	8.65
Middle rate	5.50
Lower rate	2.75

Reduced earnings allowance (under IID)

	£
Maximum rate	26.88

• Invalidity Benefit.

Invalidity allowance	£
Higher rate	8.65
Middle rate	5.50
Lower rate	2.75
Basic invalidity pension	41.15

Additional invalidity pension payable under Invalidity
Benefit depends upon your contributions to the State
Earnings Related Pension Scheme (SERPS) since April
1978.

• Mobility Allowance. This is payable to a person qualifying
as disabled who needs financial assistance to get up and
about and is currently £23.05

• Pneumoconiosis, byssinosis and miscellaneous diseases
benefit scheme.

Total disablement allowance

£

67.20

Partial disablement allowance

24.75

- Severe Disablement Allowance.

24.75

- Sickness Benefit.

Over pension age   39.45

Under pension age   31.40

- Social Fund Payments. Funeral payment is made for up to the cost of a simple funeral. The Social Fund also exists to help with discretionary payments for exceptional expenses. The DHSS determine what is an exceptional expense and whether they will assist.
- Widows Benefits.

Widows Payment (lump sum)

£

1000.00

Widows Allowance   57.65

Widowed Mothers Allowance (payable if the death of an only supporting child occurs to a widow)

41.15

Widows Pension (standard rate)

41.15

- Retirement Pension.

Basic pension based on your NI contributions

£

24.75

Non-contributory (based on a man's contributions before 5 July 1948).

Full rate   24.75

Over 80s addition   0.25

Over 80s pension   24.75

- Unemployment benefit.

People over state pension age

£

41.15

People under state pension age
32.75

If you want more detailed information you can ring Free-line Social Security – a free and confidential service on 0800 666 555. There are many useful leaflets at your local social security office and sometimes in your local post office, library and Citizens' Advice Bureau. If you are in straightened circumstances please contact your social security office, you cannot know whether you are eligible for financial help unless you ask.

Further assistance

There are other sums of money that you might be entitled to, too, before we can move on to the business of budgeting.

Home improvement grants are available from local authorities to upgrade old or dilapidated dwellings, subject to certain conditions. For example, you may be able to obtain a grant to insulate your loft if your house is old and has no insulation at all; or to replace your roof, or install proper plumbing and bathrooms, if your house is over 100 years old. If you live in a listed building (one that is protected by the local authority from demolition or structural alteration because of its historical interest) you may be able to arrange grants to help you do repairs to the essential fabric of the building. The only problem with grants is that they vary in availability from council to council. If you live in an area that has a lot of old buildings, the council may run out of grant money very quickly and you will have to wait until next year.

There are certain charities that will help individuals in financial distress, such as the Distressed Gentlefolk's Association and some of the Armed Service organisations. Again, you can find out about these from your local Citizens' Advice Bureau.

In terms of other help, as I mentioned in the previous chapter, there is the home help service, and there is also meals-on-wheels. If you are disabled or infirm you are entitled to free home nursing visits and free chiropody. Most social services departments will install aids for the disabled and elderly free of charge and they may even pay towards the cost of a yearly holiday, or provide some free holiday facility. The WRVS run many free or minimal charge facilities such as clothing funds and luncheon clubs. There are many places to turn to if you need help.

Once you are certain of your entitlements you can make a proper assessment of your financial situation.

ASSESSING THE INCOMINGS AND OUTGOINGS

Take a large sheet of paper and write on the top left-hand side 'Income'. Underneath this heading list any of the items below which bring you in an income:

Salary (full-time)
Salary (part-time)
Interest on savings
Interest on shares
Student grant
Allowance from parents
Tips
Commission
Holiday job
State retirement pension
Private employment pension

Services pension (Army, etc.)
Rent from lodgers/holiday
   lets
Profit-sharing scheme
Royalties
Trust income
Company bonus (if it's a
   regular, guaranteed one)
Repayments on loans you
   have made
Other rent (say on a garage
   you rent out)
Disability pension from work
State benefits
Annuity payments.

On the top right-hand of the page write the heading 'Expenses' and list underneath that heading any of the items below that are applicable:

Rent
Rates
Mortgage
Ground rent
Service charges
Gas
Electricity
Other heating expenses
  (paraffin, bottled gas, etc.)
Water rates
Communal heating charges
  (in rented accommodation)
Car tax
Car insurance
Car maintenance
Car MOT
Life insurance
Mortgage indemnity
  insurance
Building insurance

House contents insurance
Food (including toiletries,
  etc.)
Drink (meaning alcohol)
Fares to and from work or
  college
Meals out (from staff canteen
  lunches to evenings out)
Club fees
Alimony payments
Maintenance/child support
  payments
Investments
TV rental
Video rental
Telephone
Health insurance
Pension plan
Domestic help wages
Savings

This last item can be used as a catch-all to embrace money spent on holidays, new furniture, entertainment, etc. In other words all the things you have to do without if you cannot afford them this year.

Break down all your income amounts and expense amounts into monthly sums. In other words, if you pay approximately £50 a quarter for your telephone rental then round it up to £60 (it helps if you overestimate expenditure) and break it down to the monthly sum of £20. If you are paid a weekly wage, then add it up to the monthly total and put that down and so on. Then write the relevant sums by the relevant items as in Figure 1.

Figure 1 INCOME VERSUS EXPENDITURE FOR MRS A, A WIDOW AGED 47

Income (£ per month)		Expenditure (£ per month)	
Salary (part time)	380.00	Rates	18
(before tax)		Water rates	7
Savings interest	5.00	Gas	20
Tips	30.00	Electricity	20
Catalogue commission	25.00	Fares	20
Widows pension	164.60		
(before tax)		Bldg. insurance	8
		Contents insurance	6
		Food	100
		Drink	30
		TV rental	20
		Telephone	15
		Savings	50
		Health insurance	50
		Golf club fee	10
		HP repayments	30
Gross income	604.60	Total expenditure	404
Net income	509.16*		

*This person is allowed to earn approximately £217.83 per month without paying tax. The interest on savings has already had tax deducted therefore that leaves a balance of £381.77 each month that is liable for 25% tax deduction. That means that approximately £95.44 would be deducted, leaving the net income each month of £509.16.

As you can see from Figure 1, Mrs A. has a healthy surplus income of £105.16 each month.

What you also need to do is an annual cashflow projection, which will show the periods when you are likely to have a lot of bills coming in and how long you are likely to have in between to put money aside for the tough months. It should look like Figure 2.

Figure 2 CASHFLOW FORECAST

		JAN	FEB	MAR	APR	MAY	JUN	JUL	AUG	SEP	OCT	NOV	DEC
1.	MORTGAGE/RENT	•	•	•	•	•	•	•	•	•	•	•	•
2.	RATES	•	•	•	•	•	•	•	•	•	•	•	•
3.	WATER RATES				•						•		
4.	GAS		•			•			•			•	
5.	ELECTRICITY		•			•			•			•	
6.	TELEPHONE	•			•			•			•		
7.	HP REPAYMENTS	•	•	•	•	•	•	•	•	•	•	•	•
8.	TV/VIDEO RENTAL	•	•	•	•	•	•	•	•	•	•	•	•
9.	HOUSE INSURANCES			•(BUILDINGS)						•(CONTENTS)			
10.	OTHER INSURANCES	•(PRIVATE HEALTH SCHEME)				•(LIFE)							
11.	CAR EXPENSES (TAX, INSURANCE)			•(TAX)			•(INSURANCE)		•(TAX)				
12.	CAR RUNNING COSTS (PETROL, SERVICE, MOT)				•(SERVICE)						•(SERVICE & MOT)		
13.	FARES	•	•	•	•	•	•	•	•	•	•	•	•
14.	CREDIT CARD REPAYMENTS												•
15.	MISCELLANEOUS												
16.	"												
17.	"												
18.	TOTALS												

(a) The cashflow forecast not only gives a forecast of expenditure but, as you fill in the amounts, it will also give you a historical record of expenditure. The purpose of the cashflow forecast is to identify heavy months of expenditure so that you can be prepared.

(b) The headings would obviously be different to suit your particular circumstances.

(c) The starting month can be at any time during the year.

(d) The table can be filled in with actual amounts or estimates. You may know what certain amounts will be, but others will have to be estimated by adding 10% on to last year's bill for the same heading. That is, if last year's rates were £50 a quarter, make this year's rates £55.

(e) You will not be able to fill in the miscellaneous sections in advance since these will cover unexpected amounts such as car repair, etc.

(f) As time goes by your forecasting will become more accurate as you will be able to refer back to previous year's forecasts.

Of course, your budget and your yearly cashflow projection may be totally different to the above examples. You may not be a salaried person at all, you may be a student or a retired person with no mortgage left to pay. Whatever your circumstances, the point is that you should have enough money coming in in the Income column to meet the outgoings in the Expenditure column with, hopefully, a bit left over for rainy days and holidays. By breaking down the quarterly or annual outgoings into monthly amounts you will see exactly how much money you have to set aside every month to meet those periodic demands on your cash.

Matching income and expenditure

If your income does not exceed your expenditure, then you must isolate items on your expenditure list first of all, to see if they can be reduced. For example, the food bill, are you spending unwisely? This may not be the case, be realistic about your needs: do not skimp on food or heating or you may put your life at risk in the winter. It may be possible to boost your income rather than diminish your expenditure.

Be realistic about your situation. If you are sitting in a very large house on your own, which is draining away your resources because it still has mortgage payments to be met and it takes a lot of money to heat and light every year, you must seriously consider cashing in on your assets by moving to a smaller house that eliminates your mortgage and cuts down on running costs, or by taking out an annuity on your house.

An annuity is an arrangement with a financial institution whereby, if you are over retirement age and do not want to leave your property to anyone when you die, they will effectively buy your house from you (albeit at a bit less than the market price), give you guaranteed security of tenure until you die, and turn the money that they pay you for the house into a regular income for life. These schemes have rejuvenated many elderly people's lives and effectively eliminated money worries.

If you are younger, perhaps living alone after the death of an elderly parent, and you are in the same situation of having a large house or flat that is too much of a financial burden for you, then you must either sell or take in lodgers. Although this may be unwelcome, particularly if you are very fond of the place in which you live, the alternative may be that you spend the next few years in a state of anxiety and misery because of money worries. As the previous chapters in this book show you can make a marvellous home for yourself somewhere else, providing you choose with care.

If you are renting accommodation, and suspect that the rent is too high, you can apply to a rent tribunal to have it reduced. Rates can be queried and even contested through a rate tribunal. In practice, few people are successful in getting their rates reduced. You have to present a case based upon comparison with similar properties in the same area. However, you can get a rebate if you are on a low income. The proposed 'poll tax' will supposedly, be a fairer system for those who live alone, since they will pay, overall, less than a family living in a similar property.

If you are working, then how about looking for a job that pays more or a job that pays the same but reduces your travelling costs? Or, asking your employer if you can change your hours of work so that you can take advantage of cheap rate travel. Merely by working from ten o'clock until six o'clock instead of nine to five, workers living 10 miles from London can save half their travel costs per week.

Or, if you are young and fit enough, how about taking a second job at weekends, or some evenings? Perhaps just for a while to tide you over a particularly bad crop of bills. Evening work can be had in fast-food chains, cinemas, theatres, pubs, discos, restaurants, garages, and sometimes supermarkets. If you have a skill – typing or knowledge of motor mechanics, for instance – try advertising locally for weekend work. Simple things like window cleaning or car washing can be quite lucrative. Craft work, such as hand-knitting or celebration cake decorating, can sell quite well.

BEING THRIFTY Some of the ways in which you can be thrifty with food will be covered in the next chapter and energy management discussed in Chapter 3, should make a significant difference to your heating bills in the winter.

There are many other ways of being thrifty. For example, although in the last chapter I advocated a policy of not hoarding, there are certain exceptions. If you save every plastic container that comes into the house – margarine tubs, yoghurt pots – there is no need to buy plastic containers for the freezer or proper flowerpots. I even save tins! I have a tin-opener that cuts off the whole top of the tin under the rim and leaves a blunt edge. I save the tins, wash them and paint the outsides and I use them as cache pots for all my plants, which neatly disguises the yoghurt pots in which I have planted them!

You can also save paper and plastic bags and use them again and again for lunch sandwiches. (Making and taking your own lunches to work is a very big saving in itself.)

There are also more important economies. The telephone. Ask for a tariff of telephone charges from British Telecom. This will show you just how much you can save on your bill if you make calls out of peak periods. Invest, if you have enough money, in a telephone logging device (they start at around £30), which will tell you how long and how much each phone call you make actually costs. It will enable you to challenge telephone bills if you think they are wrong and to gain a better idea of how much you are paying while you talk. Do not stop using the telephone altogether, it is important that you maintain social contacts, but how about occasionally writing a letter instead? You can say as much as you like in a letter and it will not cost you any more than the price of a stamp.

Look hard at your outgoings and see if you can eliminate any luxuries without making yourself too miserable. Will you be happy without a video? Would it be more sensible in the long run to buy a second-hand television rather than to keep renting one? How many clubs do you subscribe to that you never really visit? How many magazines do you subscribe to at which you hardly glance? Do you take more newspapers each day than you need and do you really need them to be delivered? If you have your hair done once a week could you set it yourself and just visit the hairdressers for a cut every two months? If you smoke could you give it up to save money? Do you feed your pet on unnecessarily expensive food or could you buy a cheaper alternative? If you grow houseplants try propagating your own from cuttings rather than buying more. The same goes for the garden. Make your own plants, take cuttings or divisions from neighbours' plants, rather than buying them from nurseries. Having flowers in the house is lovely, but if you buy fresh flowers every week it is rather expensive: artificial flower arrangements might be a good alternative.

Little economies when they are added up, come to quite a lot of money each month. The above are only a few ideas; really the best person to plan for you, because you know your situation, is always you yourself.

BEWARE OF OVER-ENTHUSIASTIC FINANCIAL ORGANISA-TIONS The only way to keep control of money is by handling it yourself. I always prefer to pay all my bills by cheque or by hand.

The method of keeping little tins in the house marked 'rent', 'rates', 'telephone', etc., into which you put money may give a certain amount of satisfaction as a way of saving, but it will also give a burglar a certain amount of satisfaction to have everything so conveniently marked and to hand for him. Never stash money in the house – either in little tins, jars or under the mattress except for a small amount for use in emergencies. If you want to divide your money into separate bill categories have a post office book for each category. Take all your books and pay the necessary amounts into them, at intervals. It may not make you very popular with the queue behind you in the post office, but if it helps you that does not matter.

Direct debits or standing orders are liable to make money disappear from your account stealthily, which may be very confusing. Hidden charges on bank accounts are not helpful to anyone trying to see what is happening to their money. Unfortunately it is becoming more and more difficult to avoid things like direct debits, particularly if you are dealing with insurance companies who, on the whole, prefer this form of payment, and will try to coerce you into doing it. Legally, you cannot be forced to pay your bills by direct debit but a company may not be willing to have your business if it conflicts with its administrative practices.

It is completely untrue to say that there is no such thing as being over-insured, this is a nonsense. Insurance is only valuable if it serves a purpose. For example, the retired single person with no surviving family has absolutely no need of life assurance, since there is no one to benefit on his or her death. Health insurance, yes, but not life insurance. The difference between assurance and insurance is that the former is a guarantee under contract to pay money on the death of a named person or, in some cases, earlier during the person's lifetime, and the latter is an undertaking by an insurance company to, in return for regular premiums, undertake the risks of repaying cash for any loss or damage.

There are various reasons for taking out either or both insurance and assurance.

House Insurances
- Building insurance. Most lenders of money, e.g. banks and building societies, insist that a home owner takes out an insurance for the worth of the building, to protect it against being accidentally destroyed. It should cover fixed outbuildings, but, as many people found out during the hurricane of 1987, it does not cover fences.
- Mortgage indemnity insurance. This is an insurance that repays the mortgage in full should the person paying the mortgage die.
- House contents insurance. This insures your furniture, carpet, clothes, in fact anything authorised to be in the house, against damage or theft. *Authorised* is important because there was a famous case of an insurance company turning down a claim for a fitted kitchen damaged by fire

when they discovered that a motorbike was in the kitchen at the time.

- Maisonette indemnity insurance. This is required for owners of flats. Most simply the insurance protects the value of your home against any action by another flat dweller in the block that may devalue your property. If, for example, your downstairs neighbour allows his flat to become damp and infested with woodworm so that it affects your flat, you can claim against this insurance.
- Valuables insurance. If you keep valuables in the house, such as jewellery or silver, you need a special insurance and a professional valuation of the objects.

Life Assurance (this is broken up into three basic types)
- Term assurance. This covers a person's life for a specified term. It *is not* a form of saving, as you lose the premium money if you survive the term.
- Endowment assurance *is* a form of saving as your life will be covered for a fixed term and, at the end of it, you will be paid a fixed amount, plus bonuses. Many people use this form of assurance as a method of financing a house purchase, in other words a building society will accept the policy as a guarantee of repayment of the capital sum at the end of the term, meanwhile you pay interest payments each month to the building society.
- Whole life assurance. This policy does not have a fixed term, but lasts throughout the whole of a person's life, paying out to beneficiaries after his or her death.

Car Insurance (a legal requirement, the only option you have is which type of cover to take).
- Third Party, Fire and Theft. This is the legal minimum cover you can have. It covers damage to a car that you may damage, damage to the driver of that car, and damage to your car in the case of fire or theft. It does not cover your car for damage in an accident, therefore it is usually the sort of policy taken out by people with old cars.
- Comprehensive. Everything is covered under this policy,

including claims for damage when your car is being driven, with your permission, by someone else.

- 'Off the Road' policies (the names may vary) are policies taken out by self-employed people, business executives, and salesmen – in fact anyone to whom a car is vital. They can cover the cost of car rental while your car is out of action and, for a price, they can even cover chauffeur-driven car hire or taxis if you should lose your licence.

Motor insurance policy premiums should reduce over several years if you accrue 'No claims bonuses' – in other words if you do not make any claims for damage, etc.

- It is compulsory to insure motorbikes but not pedal cycles, although insurance is available.

Health insurance
This comes in many packages so, as with all insurance, shop around. You can cover yourself for certain kinds of private medical treatment, including hospital stays, and you can cover yourself so that you will receive an income if you should fall sick and not be able to work. In some policies you can elect to do both and in others, you only receive the income if you take NHS treatment instead of private. There are exceptions. Health insurance companies will not cover alcohol or drug related illnesses or psychiatric care. Neither will they cover, what they call a 'pre-condition', that is, some illness or disability that existed before you took out the policy. Maternity or dentistry is not usually covered. There is often an upper age limit set for policyholders, although, in recent years the insurance companies have extended upwards a little. Usually they will not accept anyone over the age of 70. Anyway, the premiums become progressively expensive as one grows older.

Accident insurance
This usually covers death, loss of limbs or eyes, permanent disablement, temporary disablement and expenses for hospital stays.

Income protection insurance
It is possible for you to insure against loss of income through disablement or illness, but not against redundancy.

Domestic animal insurance
This is a kind of life and health insurance combined that covers replacement cost through death (which can be up to £3000 in the case of a horse), theft or straying, and the cost of veterinary bills.

Appliance insurance
Cookers, washing machines, storage heaters, microwaves, dishwashers, tumble dryers, refrigerators, freezers (including contents), music centres, videos, cleaners, and televisions, in other words domestic appliances are all eligible for appliance insurance.

Personal money and credit cards
It is possible to cover yourself up to a specified limit, for the loss or theft or fraudulent use of money and credit cards. Cover is usually for the United Kingdom and abroad.

Travel insurance
Travel insurance will cover theft or loss of baggage, medical expenses abroad, loss or theft of valuables/money/travellers cheques, and unavoidable cancellation of your holiday.

The list above covers the main insurance categories. There are various packages under various names. It really is important to shop around and read the fine print to find the best deal. For example, with health insurance you must compare all the benefits that the different companies offer, because they can be markedly different.

In the end, it is possible, technically, to insure against any risk. You can make a private deal with insurance companies to insure your legs for a million pounds if they are your sole way of earning a living!

BANKING ARRANGEMENTS

When you live alone, where you keep your money and how you can reach it, is exceptionally important, because you do not have a live-in partner to borrow from if you have not been able to go to the bank. Borrowing money from colleagues at work, petty cash, or from neighbours is a fast way of making yourself unpopular.

Ease of access to money has been transformed recently with the introduction by building societies of cheque accounts. This means you can have the advantage of a bank account, viz. cheque book, statements, automatic cash dispensers, with the added advantage of accruing interest on any monies in your building society account and being able to pay in or withdraw money on Saturday mornings. Many of the building societies have also linked together so that their cash dispenser machines are networked. This means that you can apply for a special plastic card that will enable you to withdraw money from any of the participating societies' dispensers. This is very useful if you are travelling around.

Some of the banks have now installed machines which not only dispense cash but also accept payments. Some of the banks still have the disadvantage of being closed on Saturdays, but others, such as the TSB, now open for business on Saturday mornings. (The TSB also offers 24 hour banking through its Speedlink telephone service.)

Throughout the book I have extolled the virtues of the post office, mainly because, even in the most rural areas you are likely to have a sub post office, where you will be able to deposit and withdraw money all week and on Saturday mornings as well. The Post Office, of course, operates its own cheque account scheme – Giro – which means that you can have full bank facilities.

Another useful alternative is the Co-operative Bank, which gives you banking facilities in the various Handybanks in large Co-op stores, but also enables you to cash cheques in modest Co-op stores, anytime that the store is open.

Where you have your main account depends very much on where you are most of the time. If, for example, you work in a town and live outside the town, it makes sense to have your account near your place of work, then you can sort out any problems, or have interviews with your bank manager during your lunch hour. If you had your account in a bank near to your home, it would mean taking time off work to deal with money problems.

It is important, however, to have a source of money close to home. Within walking distance, if you can, and one that can be tapped at weekends.

Although I have stressed that one should not keep large amounts of money at home, it is of value to have at least a small amount of emergency money carefully hidden somewhere in the house, say, £20. In a period of very bad weather, for example, especially in a rural area the post office may run out of real cash, as might other shopkeepers, after a few days without contact from the outside world.

Where you keep the major portion of your money also depends upon what additional services you are like to require from your 'bank'. If you feel that, over the years, you might wish to avail yourself of some loans for home improvement, a new car, or some major item of expenditure, then you really do need to keep favour with a bank. Also you may have a lot of standing orders or direct debits, with which, although building societies are becoming more accustomed to dealing, banks still have more experience in administering.

You may want a permanent overdraft facility. This is extremely useful if you are self-employed and your cashflow fluctuates. All banks now offer 'budget accounts', which are a form of savings and overdraft system, whereby you undertake to allow the bank to transfer a set sum from your main account into the budget account each month. This accumulates and is used to pay bills. If there is any money in the account it earns some interest, if it goes into the red you pay some interest. For some people it is a useful way of letting the bank take the strain of dealing with bills, others prefer to handle their own budget.

Bank and building society managers are supposed to be approachable: if yours is not then change to another branch.

It may be essential for you to have a sympathetic ear if you run into difficulties.

DEALING WITH DEBT

Hopefully you will never be in this situation if you have made a realistic appraisal of your incomings and outgoings and taken measures to raise the former and reduce the latter. However, it is very easy to find yourself in a financial crisis. You could receive a lot of heavy bills which you had not anticipated, or you might suffer a car accident and find that the other person is not insured, or if your spouse has died you may be left with debts that you were unaware of.

It may distress you deeply, especially if you have never been in debt before, but do not succumb to anxiety. Here is one way to take remedial action.

1. Add up all your debts to determine the total figure.
2. Work out how much money you have to spare each month.
3. Divide the total figure of the debts by the amount of your spare cash each month, e.g. Total debt £350; total spare cash each month £25. Divide £350 by £25 = 14. Therefore you would be able to pay the debt off over fourteen months.
4. If the debt is all owed to one organisation then you must write to them, explain your problem and offer to pay off the debt in fourteen instalments.
5. If the debt is divided between several organisations, then you must calculate what you can afford to pay each organisation out of your £25 spare a month; e.g.
Fred Bloggs builders	£10 per month for 14 months
Sid Smith carpenter	£10 per month for 14 months
Eric Brown glazier	£5 per month for 14 months

Most organisations owed money would rather make such an arrangement, and have their money back eventually, than run the risk of saying goodbye to the money altogether. Certainly, the Gas Board, Electricity Board, local authorities (rates and rents) and Water Board are sympathetic towards people who wish to clear their debts in this way. They all have people who deal specifically with debt problems and will be happy to sit down and talk to you. It is worth considering, in order to help avoid debt problems cropping up, to apply to these organisations for a monthly payment arrangement anyway. It is possible to pay your rates monthly, rather than in one big lump sum and to have a 'budget account' with the Gas and Electricity Board who estimate your likely yearly consumption, based on the number of appliances you have, and work out a monthly payment figure. If, at the end of the year, you have used less power than they estimated, then they credit your overpayment to your next year's account. Building societies will, generally, be sympathetic if you ask to suspend your mortgage payments for a fixed period because you have been made redundant or because you have a crisis. They just add the period lapsed on to the end of your mortgage term. But you must inform them in writing of the situation. Do not just avoid paying the bills in the hope that you will eventually find the money. Some mortgage protection policies will give you a breathing space if you are made redundant, but most just cover mortgage repayments in the event of accident or death.

It is the small local business, as in the examples above of builders, carpenters and glaziers, who are most likely to balk at long-term clearance of a debt. Again, you have another alternative. Go to your bank manager and explain your problem, he or she will probably be able to advance you the money to pay these people off straight away and you will then pay the bank the £25 a month, except that because you will pay interest, it will probably take you sixteen months to pay it off instead of fourteen.

If a very close relative offers to lend you the money in return for an interest-free repayment of the loan, take up the offer, if you know that he or she genuinely will not miss the money. Do not be tempted to borrow from friends or neighbours, no matter how desperate you are. Many friendships have soured because the friend or neighbour has lost patience with the protracted repayment and starts becoming difficult to deal with. And never borrow money from a moneylender (or specialist finance or credit company, as they are usually called) who charges interest way above the odds, otherwise you will be paying off the debt over two years rather than fourteen months. The small print on the contracts is often confusing and you can end up paying more than you thought for longer than you anticipated.

The main thing is to communicate with your creditors. Never evade their letters or telephone calls, it will only make them less amenable to your predicament. It is also important to discuss your problem with someone. Keeping quiet and worrying about it is a bad policy. There are many people to whom you can turn for help. The Citizens' Advice Bureaux are used to helping people sort out their debt problems. If you are elderly or disabled and have regular contact with your social services department, they may be able to help you with loans or with support. Often, these people will write letters for you to your creditors, to add that little bit of official weight.

If you are a student, then go to your student welfare officer and explain your problems. A working person can often obtain help from their employer, in the form of advances on their salary, particularly if the debt problem has arisen through unforeseen circumstances and not just through their own negligence.

5·EATING FOR ONE – OR MORE

Food is all things to all people. It can be a comfort, although you should take care not to let it be a thoughtless source of comfort, it can be a creative outlet (I love creating special dishes), it can be a source of pride, and it can be a pleasure.

Just because you live alone does not mean that you should not bother. If you always eat out, or live out of tins, you are missing a whole activity of self fulfilment in life. A bachelor friend of mine takes great pride in culinary art which leaves him never short of admiring girlfriends. Another friend of mine spends her whole time, since her retirement, experimenting with different recipes. Every letter I receive from her contains a recommendation to try this or that recipe.

Of course it can be difficult, when you work or study all day, to arrive home at about seven o'clock and try to feel enthusiastic about preparing a meal. In the same way when you are elderly and live alone, it may seem like too much bother to cook just for yourself. And for disabled people, too, cooking can be such an effort of organisation, that they are sometimes tempted not to do anything.

As I said in earlier chapters, though, when you live alone two things are very important – firstly that you love and take care of yourself, and secondly, that you give yourself a treat now and then. Even if you only cook properly at weekends, it is something, and you must not neglect your health by eating processed foods all the time or by skipping meals altogether.

Although there are some marvellous cookery books for single people – Delia Smith's 'One is Fun' is a good example – I have always found that the trick is not to cook for one, but to cook for four, or whatever the recipe you are following suggests, and to freeze the rest for further meals. That way, you only make the effort to prepare and cook the meal once, and for the other three meals you just pull something out of the freezer and heat it up.

THE FREEZER

There is no need to have an enormous freezer, in fact it is better if you do not, unless you grow a lot of garden produce. A small freezer attached to a fridge will do.

A freezer will also help you to save money, providing you do not keep filling it with expensive exotic ice creams or whole sides of beef. A freezer should be there for you to maximise on your budget by storing economically prepared foods such as soups and stews, and for storing either your own garden produce or purchases of vegetables and fruits when they are at their cheapest. The other advantages of a freezer are that it enables you to store food that can be brought out in an emergency when you have unexpected guests, or to store certain foods in bulk, such as bread, to save you from frequent trips to the shops.

Freezing food

The following is a guide to what foods can be frozen and their storage lives:

Item	Storage life (months)	Item	Storage life (months)
Meat		Sausages	1
Bacon (whole)	3	Sausage meat	1
(sliced)	1	Veal	2
Beef	12		
(minced)	2	*Poultry*	
Ham	3	Chicken	12
(sliced)	1	Duck	6
Lamb	9	Giblets	3
Offal	2	Goose	6
Pork	6	Poultry stuffing	1
Roast meats	1	Turkey	6

Game		Precooked meals	
Feathered game	10	Curries	2
Hare	6	Fish dishes	2
Rabbit	6	Meat in sauce	2
Venison	12	Pizzas	1
		Souffles	2
Fish		Stews	2
Oily fish	2		
Shellfish	1	Vegetables	
White fish	6	Asparagus	9
		Brussel sprouts	10
Dairy Produce		Carrots	10
Butter (fresh)	6	Chips (part fried)	4
Cheese (soft)	6	Fresh herbs	10
(hard)	3	Green beans	12
Cream (double)	6	Peas	12
Eggs	12	Spinach	12
Ice cream	3	Tomatoes	6
Cakes, Pastries and Puddings		Fruit	
Biscuits (unbaked)	4	Apricots	6
Cakes (decorated)	3	Cherries	7
(plain)	6	Currants	10
(unbaked)	2	Fruit juices	9
Danish Pastries	1	Fruit purees	5
Fruit pies	6	Gooseberries	10
Mousses	2	Melon	9
Pancakes	2	Peaches	6
Pastry (baked)	3	Plums	6
(unbaked)	3	Raspberries	12
Souffles	2	Rhubarb	12
Sponge puddings	3	Strawberries	12
Breads		Miscellaneous	
Bread (baked)	2	Pasta (undercooked)	1
(unbaked)	2	Pate	1
Breadcrumbs	3	Sauces	2
Sandwiches	2	Soup	2
		Stock	2

There are plenty of books available on the subject of freezing. Suffice it to say, here, that freezers really are a good investment. So much so that several social services departments in the United Kingdom are now issuing their elderly and disabled meals-on-wheels customers with small freezers and a week's supply of meals for them to store and heat up themselves. This gives the customers some choice about what they will have for each meal, and when they have it.

Even if you do fill your freezer with packaged ready-made meals (and there are some very good ones now, even if they are a little expensive), it at least saves you time and organisation.

YOUR STORE CUPBOARD

Preserving

There are other methods of storing food such as preserving, drying, or bottling, but these are of limited value if you live on your own, since, even if you entertain a lot, you would probably waste a lot of preserves or bottled food, as their condition quickly deteriorates once the jar or bottle is opened. I once visited a pensioner in my village and mentioned that I occasionally like jam but never make it myself because I do not eat it often enough. He looked at me glumly and said 'I know what you mean. My sister makes lots of preserves and she's always giving me some.' Whereupon he opened a huge cupboard which was filled from top to bottom with home-made jams, marmalades, chutneys, and pickles – some of which were five years old!

Two storage items that are really useful are a brine crock and a rumtopf.

A brine crock is great for storing runner beans for a really long time. Put layer after layer of washed, fresh runner beans and plenty of salt in a large-necked earthenware container, cover the neck with a cloth and put it in a cool, dark place. After a while the salt and the moisture from the beans forms a powerful brine that perfectly preserves the beans. Whenever you want some, you just grab a handful out of the crock, wash them thoroughly, and you have delicious beans ready for cooking.

A rumtopf is the same sort of thing, in other words an earthenware container, but it usually has a lid on, and its purpose is to preserve soft fruits in alcohol. Put any combination of any soft fruits you like into the rumtopf and cover each layer with rum or brandy, so that the fruit is thoroughly soaked, and then forget about it until the winter. Your dinner parties will be legendary for their incredible desserts!

General Storage

I keep everything loose in glass jars (you can wash and save any that you buy), which prolongs their life, rather than leaving them in the packets. A basic storage cupboard should probably contain:

Rice (long grain and short grain – easiest to cook)
Pasta (several varieties)
A mixture of dried pulses (for soups)
Tea
Coffee
Sugar
Salt (a very large container – useful for icy front doorsteps as
    well as a condiment)
Tinned and dried fruit
Some tinned or bottled vegetables such as baked beans, peas,
    green beans, tomatoes, etc.
Packet sauces (transform any meal quickly)
Stock cubes (meat, vegetable and fish)
Dried herbs
Bottled sauces (tomato, savoury, soy)
Mustard
Bottled pickles
Tins of ready-made curry sauce
Tinned fish (pilchards, sardines, mackerel fillets, tuna, etc.)
Flour
Olive oil and vegetable oil
Biscuits
Crackers and crispbread
Nuts (whole and chopped)
Tomato puree

Jam, marmalade, syrup, honey and mincement
Tins of soup
Tinned ham and corned beef.

A well-stocked storage cupboard, combined with a freezer, should see you through any emergency brought about by weather or illness, for example. Replacing every item as you use it is a sure way of always being prepared – and of being certain what you have in the house.

BUYING FRESH PRODUCE

There is little to say about this except that if living alone is a new experience for you you will tend to buy too much at first and waste a lot unless you cook and freeze. The way to guard against this really is to buy little and often. Too frequently I have made the mistake of buying fresh food once a week and either running out of organisational steam halfway through the week, so all the meals I had planned to cook have fallen by the wayside, or being held up at work or in some other way and grabbing fish and chips on the way home instead. Either way half the food I had bought at the weekend was wasted.

If you are unused to living alone you will also find that you cook too much food. Try to discipline yourself to using up leftovers. I have a dog, which helps. She is happy to eat leftover mashed potato and positively loves rice pudding! Leftovers can well be used again in your own meals though, and are so good that they are even marketed these days. 'Bubble and Squeak' (mashed potato, onion and cabbage) is the simplest meal on earth to make.

I often use up leftover vegetables in a vegetable omelette or as part of a rice-based meal, a sort of risotto. That is why rice and pasta are such useful things to have in the store cupboard, because you can mix them with anything. A plate of spaghetti mixed with a fried courgette and some fried mushrooms, covered with a packet cheese sauce takes only fifteen minutes to prepare. Using leftovers and store cupboard items, you will have made a meal that many people pay several pounds for in restaurants.

USEFUL COOKING AIDS

- The slo-cooker is a wonderful implement and my most treasured cooking pot.

  A basic slo-cooker is an earthenware pot, with a lid, set in a metal frame that contains a heating element. They come in various sizes. I now have two: I use one for savoury dishes and one for sweet dishes.

  Everything cooks very slowly in a slo-cooker because the heating element is extremely gentle and costs no more to use than leaving a light bulb switched on for a day (a few pence). The slowness of the process means that you can fill it up with all the necessary ingredients for your soup, stew, casserole, risotto, or pudding, before you go out in the morning and you will arrive home to a wonderful smell and a meal that is instantly ready. Slo-cookers make meat beautifully tender and cook perfect custards and sauces. Most dishes take about 8 to 10 hours to cook, but some foods, such as pasta, can only be added to a dish halfway through, otherwise they disintegrate.

  A good slo-cooker will come with a recipe book, but there are many recipe books that deal with slo-cooking, such as *Slow Cooking Properly Explained* by Dianne Page, or Marks and Spencer's *One Pot Cooking*.
- Food processors have revolutionised some people's lives because they take all the effort out of preparing food, as they do all the chopping, slicing, grating, blending, whisking, and kneading incredibly fast. The only disadvantage I find with them is that there are so many bits to take apart and wash and, as with most plastic bowls it is difficult to rid them of the smell of onions. In an ideal world I suppose one should have two – a sweet and a savoury – like my slo-cookers, but that is rather extravagant.
- Blenders are very useful, particularly if you make

nourishing soups in your slo-cooker and you occasionally want to puree them.

- Juice extractors are a good idea for people living alone because they enable you just to juice one orange at a time, when you fancy some juice, whereas a litre carton may well start fermenting before one person can drink it all.
- Microwaves have been adopted by busy people up and down the country. They are a boon if you have a hectic lifestyle. If you are busy or infirm, the advantage of being able to take a ready-made meal out of the freezer and put it in the microwave where it is cooked in under ten minutes, far outweighs any aesthetic pleasure that purists might derive from lengthy cooking processes.
- Finally, especially if you are living alone for the first time, invest in some small cooking dishes and fridge/freezer containers. That way you can cook and store the right amounts for a meal just for you.

FEEDING GUESTS

You will also need some larger dishes and containers for when you entertain guests.

Economical entertainment

THE GUEST WHO COMES TO STAY FOR A FEW DAYS
You *have* to know, or find out, what foods your guest likes and loathes – otherwise the entire stay will be an embarrassing misery. Then plan ahead, if you can. If a friend descends upon you unexpectedly, you just have to hope that whatever you have in the freezer will suffice. If you do not have a freezer, then you will have to shop during your guest's stay.

However, if you are given advance warning, think about the stay and about the meals you will have to provide. A typical weekend visit where the guest arrives Friday night and departs Sunday night will probably mean you have to cater for two dinners (Friday and Saturday night), two breakfasts

(Saturday and Sunday morning – maybe cooked breakfasts), two lunches (Saturday and Sunday), and one tea (early Sunday evening).

It is best to make it as trouble free as possible. Firstly, make the Friday night meal a cold one, because your guest may arrive late or you may have to go and meet your guest at the bus or railway station. Just cold meat and salad, or something similar, so you have no need to worry. Make sure you have all the breakfast options available – eggs, bacon, cereal, toast. Make a simple one-pot meal for Saturday evening dinner (like a stew in the slo-cooker, so that you are not forever preparing the meal and forever washing up). A slo-cooker, of course, will allow you and your guest to spend the whole of Saturday out and about, without worrying about the preparation of a meal when you arrive home.

If you can afford it eat out modestly over the stay; have a pub snack, for instance, on the Saturday while you are both out shopping or sightseeing, and a roast lunch on the Sunday. Eating out (particularly Sunday lunch) gives you a break from cooking and gives your guest some variety of scenery.

THE DINNER OR LUNCHEON PARTY Whatever time of day it is, this is most likely to mean inviting a group of people over for a 'sit-down' meal. The grandness of the meal, and how much of it you pay for, depends upon the expectations of yourself and your guests and perhaps their relationship to you. If, say, you are a young person – student or worker – who has invited over friends of the same age, they will probably expect to bring a bottle of wine with them. In fact, most friends, of any age, would bring a bottle of something – unless the dinner party was very grand. Relatives often seem to feel that they do not need to bring a contribution, unless, of course, you are young, living alone for the first time and being visited by your mother, in which case she will probably bring a month's supply of food and wash up for you as well!

Save your energy at both dinner and luncheon parties. If the meal is to be three courses, then make the first and last courses cold – prawn cocktail and chocolate mousse for example – prepare it the night before and put it in the fridge. Do not give yourself a nervous breakdown trying to prepare and cook three courses on the day perfectly and on time. Guests are often late and rarely sit down at the table on time. So if you have a cold starter and dessert and a main course that is either a one-pot meal, like a casserole, or a roast, where the oven temperature can be adjusted to cope with delays in starting, then you should avoid disasters.

Do not believe any articles you may read that are written by restaurateurs, professional chefs or cordon bleu cooks about either soufflés, profiteroles, or flambés being the simplest thing in the world. They are recipes for disaster when you are entertaining.

For a really cheap and cheerful gathering of friends you could do worse than invest in a fondue set and a plastic tablecloth and let everyone sit around dipping their bread into the cheese fondue, while holding a glass of nice wine in the other hand.

If you are going to eat al fresco then I would give you two tips. Make as much of the meal cold as you can – it would only become cold between your kitchen and the garden anyway. You could perhaps introduce the occasional hot item such as garlic bread, wrapped in tinfoil, to compliment the salad, and hot fudge sauce to pour over an ice cream dessert. The second tip is that if you are planning an evening meal, do not have candles or any kind of light on the table itself. Have the lighting some distance away from the table, otherwise all your food, and you and your guests, will be covered in moths, mosquitos, and midges before you even reach to the main course.

PARTIES Parties need careful planning and handling when you live alone (See next chapter). The main thing is not to be too ambitious about the food. You cannot answer the door; take people's coats; circulate and generally be a good host/ ess, if you keep going into the kitchen.

Hot food is not feasible unless you have a hot tray, an electric fondue set, or a slo-cooker, which can all be placed on a buffet table and used for keeping things warm. Cold food even if fairly predictable can be easily and quickly topped up – crips, nuts, sausage rolls, quiche, french bread, and cheese are all adequate. Sandwiches and canapes go stale very quickly at a party. A variety of cheeses and a paté, French bread and butter are simple and popular. People will help themselves and save you a lot of work, as will buying paper plates for everyone to use and making the buffet a finger buffet with lots of little bits and pieces of food, and nothing that has to be served onto a plate with a spoon or cut up with a knife and fork.

In general people prefer finger buffets anyway, because unless you have lots of seats they invariably have to stand up and most people find it terribly difficult to eat a fork buffet standing up.

Do not forget to provide one or two items of sweet food – individual cakes or petit fours. Very creamy cakes, or gateaux are likely to deposit cream on your carpet though.

6·ANYTHING BUT LONELY

It can sometimes seem hard to be part of an active social life if you live by yourself. Entertaining is one way of enjoying a sociable occasion in your home. I am not suggesting that you throw extravagant dinner parties every night when I advocate entertaining. Inviting people into your home to partake of food and drink can be a modest invitation to one person to come and have a cup of coffee and a biscuit.

COMPANY IN YOUR HOME

There are all sorts of opportunities for this. For instance, if you are talking to a neighbour and he or she seems in no particular rush, then invite him or her in for an impromptu cup of something. I often invite people round for Sunday morning drinks – a pre-lunch sherry, for instance.

Christmas provides a good opportunity to invite neighbours and friends into your house for drinks and tit-bits. But there is no reason to restrict it to Christmas. I have always found that Sunday lunchtime is the best time to entertain. It is always the most convenient for my guests in that they do not have to drive in the dark, and they can have a much more leisurely lunch, without worrying about the time, as they would in the evening over dinner. Friends can come quite a long distance to have Sunday lunch with you, whereas for an evening dinner, there probably would not be enough time.

Also, Sunday lunches, especially in the summer, are so lovely and relaxed. One can usually have them outside, in the garden or on a patio or balcony, and the whole day can be stretched to include tea and cakes at around four o'clock.

Many people find summer tea parties with scones and strawberries served on the lawn very appealing and much more romantic than mugs of coffee and biscuits in the kitchen.

Summer is also a marvellous time to have an 'open house' day. These are marvellous opportunities to invite all sorts of people – friends, neighbours, relatives – to visit at any time between, say, eleven o'clock in the morning and ten o'clock at night. A cold buffet, which can be topped up through the day, is ideal, and people float in and out, stopping just for a drink and a few peanuts, or staying much longer. Only those with plenty of stamina can attempt an 'open day', however, since a twelve-hour stint of entertaining requires forethought and energy. Once a year is probably often enough.

When I was putting this book together, an acquaintance told me about her 'getting-to-know-the-neighbours' spaghetti parties. These simply involve inviting a handful of neighbours in for a fairly informal plate-on-your-lap spaghetti meal.

There are lots of excuses for throwing parties: your birthday; a housewarming; a new job; and so on. However, when you live alone and you are inviting comparative strangers to your party, it is wise to enlist the help of a friend beforehand to help you cope, particularly if you do not feel you could deal with evicting people who might become drunk or who overstay their welcome. You may also think that you would like help with the planning and execution of the catering. Elderly people may turn to a younger relative or friend to help them host a party.

A party, though, can just be a handful of people – you do not have to overstretch your resources or capabilities. I have had some very nice Boxing Day parties of no more than ten people. We have helped ourselves to a buffet, had a few drinks, watched television and played games, as though we were a large family.

Whatever the form of your home entertaining, always be conscious of the fact that you must control it. It must be the sort of occasion that does not cause you anxiety; cost you a fortune; or invade, rather than compliment, your home.

GOING OUT

You cannot expect the world always to come to you – you must go out and meet it sometimes if you are going to have a full social life. Going out, especially at night, may seem particularly dangerous for people on their own, but there are many things you can do to promote your safety whether you are a man or a woman.

Safety rules

- Never walk alone, day or night, across commons, waste-ground, down alleys, quiet or unlit roads, or through pedestrian subways.
- Do not expose yourself to risk by waiting alone at bus stops or by entering single or empty carriages on trains. Always sit near the door, try to sit near the driver, guard or conductor, and make a mental note of where the emergency alarm is.
- As part of your budgeting, set aside some money each month for taxi fares. Only take registered cabs home, i.e. ones that display licences in the cab and that can be telephoned to book your ride. Never accept lifts from a stranger and never use 'moonlighting' cabs, no matter how desperate you are. Never tell any cab driver, registered or not, that you live alone. If you arrive at your local station and it is just impossible to find a cab, then go to your local police station if it is close by and explain your problem. They would rather ring for a cab for you, or even give you a lift home, than have to deal with any attack that could be made on you on your lonely way home. If there is no police station to hand, go to a public place, such as a garage, and ask if you can ring for a cab.
- When walking alone, particularly at night, always be aware of all the sounds and movements around you. Do not wear a personal stereo headset so that you are unaware if someone comes up behind you. Be aware of potential trouble before you walk into it – if, for instance, there is a group of drunks

five hundred yards ahead of you cross over or take the next turning to avoid it.

- If you think someone is following you, turn into the first public place or lighted house you come to. If the person appears to be loitering, then ask the person in charge there or the householder if you can phone the police. No matter how close you are to your home, never lead a suspicious person to it so that he can see you enter an empty house/ flat alone.
- Never display anything that may tempt a thief. Women should, if possible, put their purse and cheque book in an inside coat pocket instead of carrying a handbag. A back trouser pocket is the easiest pocket both to pick, and from which to lose either money or a wallet.
- Do not wear lots of obvious jewellery when you are out. There are other, safer ways of looking glamorous or attractive and lots of gold on display is a powerful temptation to thieves or muggers.
- Always have your car or front door keys ready by the time you need them. You are very vulnerable while you are standing fumbling in your handbag or pockets. Front door keys are best not kept in a handbag anyway, because if your handbag should be stolen you will not be able to enter your house.
- If you are really nervous of being out and about, invest in a personal alarm, which you should carry in your hand at all times. These emit a piercing shriek when pressed.
- Be very careful when you withdraw money from street cash dispensers. Have a good look around before attempting the transaction. It may even be safer if elderly, infirm or disabled persons do not use high street cash dispensers, they are too easy a target for opportunistic thugs.
- Variety is important. Collect your pension on different days of the week. Vary your walk home from work as far as possible.
- If you are driving alone in a car, do not stop to pick up hitch-hikers, always lock all your doors if you are sitting in a parked car and do not roll down the window to give a

suspicious looking stranger directions. If your car breaks down and you have to leave it for help, try to stick to well-lit areas and do not accept a lift from anyone. If you break down on a motorway, do not leave your car, just wait for the motorway patrols to find you.

If you follow the above rules you should be as safe as possible. I cannot go into all the options if you should be unfortunate enough to be attacked. It is better if you attend a course which specifically deals with self-defence. Always, the best thing to do is to run and shout for help, before attempting anything else.

With this preventative action in mind there are a number of socialising options open to you.

General sociability

You do not have to immediately join a group – it may not be what you want anyway and there is more about different options later.

You can bring some variety and social contact into your life by simply going out and talking to people. Instead of merely shopping, exchange a few words with shop assistants. Go to local jumble sales and bazaars. Churches provide a focus for the community and offer valuable support and social opportunities. You could also go to local amateur dramatic performances. Members of such groups are usually very friendly and so grateful that people turn up to their performances that they are quite often there to smile and chat to visitors at the door. Go to your nearest town occasionally for a special event – a concert, a festival, or a flower show. All these things you can do by yourself, but at the same time you will be making some sort of social contact.

You could develop an interest that brings you into contact with other people, like collecting paintings or other *objet d'art*. Even if your interest only takes you on regular tours of the local antique or junk shops, it will give you some stimulation.

There are also ways of developing friends at a distance, like penfriends, for example. This is not an activity restricted to schoolchildren, there are lots of organisations abroad that are anxious to find penfriends for people of all ages. You may find yourself opening up a whole new world of exciting foreign contacts which could, eventually, lead to some charming holidays.

The most important thing in socialising is that you make the time and spend the effort to keep those friends that you *do* have. Do not say 'Oh I must get around to phoning Fred or Millie' and just keep putting it off. Make regular calls and write regular letters. Keep a note of birthdays in your diary, so that you do not forget to send your friends cards and/or presents. Make the effort to send everyone a Christmas card every year. Do not let friendships lapse. It is very easy to do so, especially if friends have moved away and you are busy.

Socialising in a group

Some people do not enjoy club activities but, many if they make the effort, find that they rather enjoy being involved with something and with other people. Only join clubs, societies, or associations if the work or activity that they pursue is *really* of interest to you, though, or it is unlikely to be a success. I joined a flower arranging society thinking 'Well I quite like flowers and it's a good way to meet people', but I found it so boring that I left after three months. I realised that I needed something that was a bit more active and fairly creative, preferably something that included both sexes. I now belong to my local drama group, which is great fun, and my local history group, which is fascinating. The place to find out about local organisations and classes is the local library.

Evening classes are a good way of meeting people, adding to your skills, having fun, and learning at the same time, without the organisational demands that a club may make upon you. Most classes are advertised in the local press, or at libraries, during the summer months, and one usually has to enrol during August for start in September. However, the same rule applies to evening classes as to joining clubs – it must be a subject that really interests you. Otherwise, after a hard day's work in the middle of winter, you will find that you cannot be bothered to make the effort to go along and you will have wasted the fees.

For the retired, many adult education institutes now run daytime classes as well. These can run all year round (with perhaps a break in July/August). My local institute also runs Saturday classes. Do not forget that for the elderly, there are day centres and pensioners' 'pop in parlours'! Day centres usually offer transport to and fro, lunch and activities. 'Pop-ins' are just for tea and a chat.

If you feel energetic, you could join exercise classes at your local sports centre, village hall or other venue. There are many of these for all age groups. Again, it is not quite like joining a club, because you simply attend, you do not have to commit yourself to anything more than that.

If you are a student, you will more than likely be spoilt for choice in the social life that revolves around your educational establishment.

An alternative to clubs and classes is voluntary work. We are a nation of voluntary workers and there are so many organisations that it is sometimes difficult to know which to choose to help. Your local library will have details of all the voluntary groups in your area and who to contact with an offer of your services. Again, the golden rule is only pick a cause that is dear to your heart.

In most areas there is a Council of Voluntary Service and most of these employ a person called a Volunteer Co-ordinator. If you do not want to actually volunteer for a specific charity but would like to offer your services generally to whoever may need them, then phone the Volunteer Co-ordinator, who will match you up with all sorts of jobs. It may be decorating a flat for a housebound person, to taking care of the cat of an elderly hospitalised lady. If you have a special skill, such as being a trained accountant, a hairdresser, or even a public relations consultant, there are always charities who can do with an honorary treasurer, an old people's home that would love some free hairdressing for their residents, or an organisation that needs a brochure or press release written. You can tell the Volunteer Co-ordinator or a specific charity exactly how much time you can give them. Be decided from the outset – they prefer that, then they know what they can expect from you. If you are working, then you may only be able to help at weekends. If you are not working, do not give up all your time to charitable work – you will be worn out, for voluntary work is a bottomless pit and those who run charities freely admit that they squeeze every last drop of help that they can out of people.

One-to-one relationships

I do not mean just dating by this; there are all sorts of relationships that you can enter into that are just on a one-to-one basis.

Be careful of becoming so involved with someone that your other social life suffers. Again, I am not just talking about romantic attachments, but also about simple friendships. Some friends can be very demanding and will not do anything unless you do it as well, or want to do everything you do.

With some friends, life can become a turgid ritual of habits. Some always go for a drink at the pub with their friends on Friday nights, some always go to Bingo on Thursday nights, and so on. Not only does this become stale after a while, but it also leaves you bereft when it stops. It may not be your decision that brings it to an end, it may be someone else's or beyond anyone's power to decide. Whatever the case if it has become too much of a habit, this can be devastating.

If you do want to enjoy a one-to-one relationship of a companionable or romantic nature there are various ways one can make contact, other people who want to do the same and they need not have marriage as an aim if that is not what you want.

ESTABLISHING CONTACTS

FRIENDSHIP BUREAUX These used to be called marriage bureaux. They are organisations (they may be run from an office or from someone's home) that seek to match up like-minded individuals. Clients fill in a form that asks all sorts of personal questions and it is analysed and 'matched' to a likely candidate for their consideration.

COMPUTER-DATING AGENCIES These are a version of the friendship bureaux that use a computer to do the matching.

SINGLES CLUBS There are two types of these. One is an actual building which holds a bar, restaurant, disco, or any combination of the three, that is there specifically for singles to patronise, the other is a group of people who are all single and form a club that has different social activities at different venues. The former can be a dubious means of meeting other single people and making friends, since it will be open to all and sundry, even people who are married and masquerade as single. There is also very little likelihood that you will achieve true friendships through this type of club as they seem to cater mostly for people who want to make one-night stands.

The latter type, the singles groups, are sometimes very successful at fostering friendships because they deliberately restrict membership to a certain category of people – for example, young professionals, graduates, or over-40s. This means that everyone has something in common with the rest of the group and it leads to a more relaxed and productive social activity. The variety of the social events undertaken by such groups means that you can select what does and does not appeal to you. If, for instance, you will not enjoy a visit to the opera, then you may prefer the next month's barn dance. The good thing about these singles clubs is that there is usually no pressure at all to form oneself into a couple. The group really does operate as a group and you can attend all the social functions without feeling that you have to pair off.

CONTACT GROUPS These are usually for people who have a particular social problem in common or have just been through a similar trauma, like divorce or bereavement. The function of these groups is not to provide any romantic possibilities (although that may happen), but to provide contact and support by introducing you to people who have similar problems to yourself. For those who have a problem and feel very isolated, these groups are a valuable way of re-introducing themselves to society. Details of such groups can be found in libraries or Citizens' Advice Bureaux.

ADVERTISEMENTS Some thirteen million lonely hearts or companionship-seeking advertisements appear in the United Kingdom every year, in publications ranging from local newspapers to national magazines and covering all age ranges. I have known of some spectacularly successful relationships that have developed through this medium, particularly amongst the elderly.

SAFETY Regardless of the physical and emotional dangers of casual sexual relationships, you should be aware of your personal safety with someone you know only slightly. Never give your full address to someone that you have just spent your first evening with. Do not invite anyone into your home until you have come to know them quite well. Until you know someone, you should beware of putting yourself into a position where you may be trapped, pestered, or embarrassed.

7·LOOKING AFTER YOURSELF

You are the only person who can take care of your health. When you do not live with anyone else there is no one to nag you about smoking, drinking, eating too much, or eating the wrong things. Neither is anyone going to fetch and carry for you when you are in bed with influenza, or be there to patch you up when you fall over, burn or cut yourself. This makes three things essential:

1. That you take the best possible care of yourself to avoid ill-health.
2. That you do not become a hypochondriac.
3. That if you do become ill you accept the fact and do everything necessary to recover.

TAKING GOOD CARE OF YOURSELF

Health Hazards

Overindulgence in food and drink is a big danger for those who live alone. Food is often a comfort to people. Initially you may cheer yourself up by having a piece of apple pie and some ice cream. Eventually, though, it will catch up with you in the form of self-loathing, as the pounds pile themselves on and you possibly curb your social life, and, moreover, endanger your health. Fat constricts the blood vessels, making your circulation bad and therefore creating problems like varicose veins. Carrying around fat puts an enormous strain on the heart.

Eliminate the temptation to turn to the food cupboard for comfort by reducing to a minimum foods that can harm you: biscuits, cakes, crisps, pies, sweets, chocolate, pizzas and even bread. (You may think this last one rather harsh but many people go through the hourly slice of bread and jam syndrome.)

Fill your home with lots of varieties of fruit – you can eat as much of that as you like. Vegetables, seeds, and some nuts are all much better for you than anything like biscuits or cake. If you are a compulsive nibbler, better you should nibble on raw carrots, sunflower seeds, and pistachio nuts than anything else. You might also try other vegetables raw, raw mushrooms or raw peas, for instance.

This is not a book about dieting, so I am not going to go into the subject in great depth. The point is that it is very easy, when you live alone, to give in to compulsion.

Alcohol is a greater danger than food because it has a more powerful effect. Very lonely people turn to the tranquillising help of alcohol particularly, according to psychiatrists, men who live alone. For most people a drink is calming. Many people would rather have a stiff drink to help them sleep, than take a sleeping tablet for their insomnia. Moderation is fine, if that is what it is and what it remains. If you find your consumption is creeping up and up, do not keep alcohol in the house. If, after removing temptation, you find it too distressing, then admit that you have a problem and need help. Go and see your doctor straight away.

Tea and coffee are also drugs, and should not be underestimated. A friend of mine in Holland runs a psycho-geriatric hospital and he says that approximately twenty per cent of the patients sent to him suffering from seeming senility, i.e. confusion, some incontinence, and anxiety attacks, are in fact suffering from prolonged overdoses of tea. Some of his patients were found to be drinking as many as 40 cups of tea a day!

The small amount of stimulant that is contained in a cup of tea or coffee will not harm you if you drink two or three cups a day. If you start edging up to ten cups a day you will become over stimulated and your heart and circulatory system will be affected. Women who suffer from painful periods should consider giving up coffee altogether, because it constricts the blood vessels in the body and makes their cramps worse.

For decades (since the First World War) society has encouraged smoking, depicting it as glamorous, soothing, attractive. In the last few years, attitudes have changed and society now expects smokers to wipe out 70 years of brainwashing overnight. It may seem unreasonable, but there is no doubt about the harm smokers do to themselves and other people. People living alone are particularly at risk if they smoke because, as I mentioned in an earlier chapter, it is a considerable fire hazard in the home.

Health promotion

Regular exercise is very important, and the best ways of exercising are walking, swimming, bicycling, and gardening. If you can, try to do some form of exercise that makes you breathe hard for about ten minutes each day. This is very good for your heart and lungs. If you are at work all the time and find fitting in regular exercise rather difficult, then invest in an exercise bike or a rowing machine. Ten minutes in the morning should keep you trim. Do not suddenly take up violent exercise after years of inactivity, or you will injure yourself. The ten minutes of hard breathing mentioned above is enough to start with.

Many people like to do exercises to music and there are plenty of options – you can go to classes, devise your own exercises to music, buy one of the exercise cassettes with accompanying wall chart or, if you have a video, buy one of the exercise videos available. Do not be too ambitious with exercises. Start off with something gentle. I have several exercise videos, some of which are ridiculously tough. The one I like best is Lizzie Webb's 'The Body Programme', which starts off very gently and incorporates exercises that any age group can attempt. The tape also gives advice on diet, health, and beauty.

Mental health is very important. You must exercise your mind each day in the same way that you do your body. Think positively about what is right with your life every day. Do not sidetrack into dwelling on what is wrong with it. A psychiatrist I spoke to when researching this book advised a list method: when you wake up, if you feel depressed or lonely, write down all the positive things about your life.

I am in good health;
I have a nice house;
I have a good job;
My dog loves me;
The sun is shining today;
and so on.

Force yourself to do it, no matter how low you feel. The effort you make to think positively is the same as the effort you make to force weak leg muscles to ride a bike: it makes you stronger in the end.

Laughter is a marvellous preventitive medicine whether you feel low or not always it does you good if you take yourself off to the nearest comedy film or show. Or read a funny book. Or phone up a cheerful friend who always makes you laugh. Go out with that friend. Have a meal out, go shopping – just go out. Go out with other people and listen to them laugh. One of the great things about watching a good comedy show or film is that people around you start laughing and you are much more likely to join in. Make an effort to join in 'fun' things. If there is a local carnival every year, go along and enjoy the costumes and the general atmosphere.

Avoiding hypochondria

Depression leads to anxiety and anxiety leads to phobias and neuroses. As was noted earlier, an estimated half a million people in this country suffer from agoraphobia (the fear of leaving their home). Many people too suffer from hypochondria (the fear that they are ill).

When you live alone it is very easy to magnify every little

ache and pain into a life-threatening illness. You should never ignore something, such as a breast lump, that you may have imagined. It is better that you should go to the doctor and feel foolish for having imagined it than ignore it and face dire consequences, because it is real. Seeing your health in perspective is the important thing. If you eat the right foods and take some exercise you will begin to understand and know your body better and you will be able to discern something that is just a muscular ache from carrying heavy shopping from a pain that you have never encountered before.

Do not spend your life taking over-the-counter medication for the slightest ache or pain. Every synthetically produced drug is toxic, taken in large enough quantities. Very often a headache or a stomach upset is a sign of your system being polluted anyway – in the same way that a hangover is because of your system trying to cope with an influx of alcohol. Taking pills or powders for headaches and stomach upsets is only adding to your system's toxicity. Try drinking lots of water instead: not eating at all for a day to clear out the system (unless you are a diabetic or have some other dietary problem); having a warm bath and a nap; going for a long walk. All these things are just as likely to rid you of a headache as taking a pill.

Laxatives, in particular, can be dangerous. Unless you are disabled and your inability to move makes you constipated, there is normally no reason why you should need laxatives. If you eat plenty of fresh fruit and vegetables (particularly apples), take some extra roughage, such as bran in some form, and exercise regularly, you should have no need for laxatives. It may be that you have been taking them for so long that you are caught up in a chemical spiral and cannot now function without them. If this is the case a two-day fast on fruit juice and water will break the cycle.

Tranquillisers, anti-depressants, or sleeping tablets should only be taken if they are really needed. During a bad crisis they may help, but when you are feeling stronger you should stop taking them. Do not stop medication such as this overnight, however, because it is possible to suffer withdrawal symptoms that panic the sufferer into taking the pills for the rest of their lives. Cut down on them gradually. Take one tranquilliser a day instead of two. Similarly with anti-depressants. If you can, cut your sleeping pills in half and take half instead of a whole one before stopping altogether.

If you are tense try some of the natural relaxant products that are available from health food stores, rather than taking drugs. There are many herbal products that can help you relax or sleep, including herbal teas which, when taken with a little honey, can give an excellent night's sleep.

When you are ill

Even the healthiest person can succumb to a new form of influenza or a virus that is prevalent locally. It is very difficult, particularly for those who work in a stuffy, over-crowded office, to which they commute on a stuffy overcrow-ded train, successfully to avoid catching cold or other viruses.

When you catch something like this, the first thing you do is give in to it. No matter what your business commitments, it is far more sensible to have one day at home in bed to recover from the worst of the virus than to struggle in to work, extending the recuperation period enormously and giving the virus to everyone else. Some viruses can be so vicious that if you do not take care of yourself for a couple of days when you first fall ill you could spend three weeks or more under par.

With any virus, going to bed, making yourself as warm as possible, sleeping and drinking plenty of fruit juice and water (not milk) is the best form of medication. This will help eliminate the virus through your urine and sweat as fast as possible. Sleep is a great help to any illness, so sleep as much as you can.

Call the doctor in, if you want to. If you are offered antibiotics remember that many of them have side-effects and can leave you feeling worse than before. Tell the doctor if you are allergic to any particular medication.

Always call the doctor if you are vomiting or have diarrhoea. In either case you can easily and very quickly dehydrate and put your life at risk. Call the doctor in if any part of your body swells up or you come out in spots or rashes. You need to know what you are suffering from in case you will have to make arrangements for a longer stay at home in bed.

Making arrangements for illness and convalescence

A key deposited with a trustworthy neighbour and the location of a telephone and address book beside the bed are invaluable at times of illness, because you can call the neighbour and doctor from your sickbed and the neighbour can let the doctor in for you.

If you have to stay long in bed, or at least at home, you will need to make arrangements so that you can cope. Firstly, you will need to ask someone to do your shopping. Prescriptions must be filled out and you will probably need plenty of fruit juices, fruit, soup, and a food supplement, such as Complan.

If you are elderly or disabled, your doctor can probably arrange for the district nurse and/or health visitor to visit to see that you are all right. It is doubtful that either of those professionals will shop for you. For this you will have to rely on friends, neighbours, or relatives, or ring the Volunteer Co-ordinator at your local Council of Voluntary Service and ask him or her whether there is someone who can shop and clean for you while you are ill. You may have other problems that need dealing with – like taking the dog for a walk, for example.

Emergency hospitalization

If you have to be hospitalized then, again, it will be necessary to organise some sort of support. If your hospitalization is sudden, say, you are struck down with appendicitis at work, ask your work colleagues to telephone the neighbour who keeps your spare key and ask him or her to check that your home is all right, look after your pet or take your pet to a local kennels or vet to be looked after, water your plants, and generally keep an eye on things. Alternatively either colleagues or neighbour could perhaps ring a relative or friend who might move into your home and take care of things while you are in hospital. Do not worry about things like night clothes and toilet things – the hospital will have everything that you could need. You will not be in a condition to care about shaving, for example, for a few days in all probability anyway. If you are worried about anything, particularly your pet or pets, then either before you go under the anaesthetic or as soon as you are conscious, ask the nurse to ring your neighbour and find out if they received your message and whether everything is all right.

Planned hospitalization

If your hospital stay is planned then you will have plenty of time to organise some help to take care of your home and other responsibilities. If you do not have a co-operative neighbour, your friends are all going to be on holiday, and you have no relatives, there are businesses that 'home sit'; your local phone directory should list them. They will either put someone in your house on a full-time basis, or they will send someone round every day to check on things. Prices will probably vary according to the amount of work they have to do.

Your home will not suffer for a couple of weeks without anyone to look after it any more than when you go on holiday. You will have to lodge your pet with someone, if you have one. Most friends or neighbours will happily take a fishtank, caged bird, or animal for two weeks, providing you give them written instructions and all the feeding, bedding and any other necessities. Dogs or cats may have to be boarded at kennels. Plants will survive quite happily if you group them all together in the bath, soak them well, and leave about an inch of water in the bottom of the bath. The humidity created by grouping together in the bath will keep them moist for quite a while.

Turn off all the heating and gas. Unless it is deep winter, it should not be necessary to turn off the cold water, particularly if you want a neighbour to come in and water plants, or run a hose from the kitchen to water the garden. Do not turn off the electricity either. Your neighbour may only be able to visit your house in the evening, and will surely need light. Equally, the electricity will be needed for an automatic switch on lights to fool burglars.

Encourage as many people as possible to visit you, when you are in hospital. They will help you not to feel isolated or depressed while you are ill and away from home. If you have no one to visit you, then you can tell the nurse that you would be grateful for a hospital visitor. These are part-time volunteers who come and visit any patients who are alone. They will chat, bring you some magazines, and run errands for you. Undoubtedly you will receive a visit from the hospital chaplain. Even if you are not religious, it is a welcome chance for social contact and the exchange of a few pleasantries with him.

Having an operation naturally entails feelings of anxiety, so talk to as many professional people as you can – doctors, nurses, the anaesthetist when he comes to visit you – to reassure yourself. With a planned hospital stay you will have been told to prepare for the operation as best as you can, perhaps by losing some weight, discontinuing any medication that you may be taking, or attempting to stop smoking. All these measures are designed to give you as trouble-free an operation as possible. You must relax as much as you can. If you are admitted the day before your operation and cannot sleep, tell the nurse and she will give you a pill.

Post-operative and convalescent care

After the operation, you may feel sick or very depressed – this is the effect of the trauma of the operation and of the anaesthetic. Knowing the cause will help you pull through it. In a few days the effects of the anaesthetic will diminish and you will feel better. Do not try and rush your recovery. Many people leap out of bed and charge about the ward on their first day after the operation only to collapse in a heap the day after that.

When you are approaching the end of your hospital stay

you will have to think about convalescence. Do not underestimate the effect that even a small operation has on your body and your nervous system. Any abdominal operation will leave you with an inability to lift or carry things for at least a month. Back and leg operations may totally immobilise you, or at least prevent you from walking up any stairs for quite a while.

It is necessary to prepare for convalescence before you go into hospital if that is at all possible. If you genuinely feel that you can cope at home, with the help of neighbours and friends, then re-arrange your home accordingly. Have the bed moved downstairs if you live in a house and, if you do not have a downstairs toilet, contact the Red Cross and arrange for the loan of a commode. Arrange beforehand with your GP for regular visits from a district nurse to change your dressings, help you bath, etc. Make sure that you have in plenty of supplies – food, drink, clean nightwear and underwear, and so on – that will eliminate the need for shopping after your operation. Before you go put everything that you will need downstairs – the television, the radio, your favourite books, your plants, the paperwork that you are going to catch up on.

If you are elderly and the operation you are having is quite major, then be realistic. Unless you can arrange for someone to come and stay with you for at least a month after your operation, you will not be able to cope. Therefore, you must arrange with the hospital for a place in a convalescent home for the post-operative phase. These are usually very pleasant places by the sea or in the country where you will be waited on hand and foot until you can cope for yourself. The National Health Service does operate its own convalescent facilities but there are also many private ones if you are covered by insurance or have plenty of money.

FIRST AID IN THE HOME

You are the only person who can take care of yourself when you have an accident, so be very, very careful around the home. Accident prevention is extremely important because there are certain situations where you will be unable to help yourself, such as if you are rendered unconscious through a fall or an electric shock. Chapter Four covers all the points so you should never find yourself in the position of having an accident and being helpless.

The First Aid Box

As for other types of accidents in which you can help yourself, it is useful to have a good first aid box handy. Keep it in the kitchen (the most likely scene of accidents) and, if you live in a two-storey or more dwelling, keep one on each floor as well. There is little point in having a first aid kit on the ground floor if you cut your foot badly upstairs.

Keep all the things listed below together in a special first aid container. Never remove them and forget to put them back, it defeats the purpose. A good first aid box should contain the following:

- Several bandages in various sizes, including a crepe bandage for sprains;
- A *small* pair of scissors that will cut in awkward little corners, etc.;
- A pack of cotton wool (a roll not cotton wool balls);
- Individually packed sterile dressings in various sizes;
- Pair of tweezers;
- Safety pins;
- Sticking plaster on a roll;
- Antiseptic lotion and cream;
- Antihistamine cream;
- Gauze.

What to do when you have an accident

If you have *injured* yourself badly, for example broken your leg, concussed, or burnt yourself, call an ambulance. Dial 999, ask for an ambulance and state clearly your name and address. Then, if you can manage to go to the front door, open it, before you pass out or feel faint, or ring a neighbour who has a key. Then lie or sit down on the nearest piece of furniture, try to keep warm and wait calmly for help to arrive.

DO NOT drink or eat anything at all. You may need an operation when you arrive at hospital, or you could pass out while drinking and choke. Shock affects the blood pressure and you should neither smoke nor drink alcohol in a state of shock as this further affects the blood pressure. If you have fractured a bone or fallen and damaged your back, do not move at all, you could make it worse. If you do not have a personal alarm then try and shout for help, or bang on the floor or wall.

If you are *bleeding* badly then try to stop the flow of blood by pressing on the wound with a large pad of cotton wool, or some clean material. Do not attempt to tie a tourniquet unless you have severed an artery and blood loss is so fast that you must stop the flow quickly. If you have to tie a tourniquet, do not keep up pressure for longer than ten minutes and allow at least one minute between re-applications. As soon as you start applying a tourniquet then write on your arm or leg with a pen the time that applications started. Do this every time you re-apply the tourniquet. That way, if you should pass out before the ambulance arrives they will know when you last applied pressure.

In any case of bleeding, try to raise the affected part of the body so that the blood flows less quickly and, if it is not a severe wound that is awaiting the attention of an ambulance crew, and you are fairly mobile, try to wash the wound thoroughly before attending to it. You must go to the casualty department of a hospital to have any wound properly looked at, as soon as possible. You will probably have to have a tetanus injection, particularly if you have wounded yourself while gardening.

If you have a *nose bleed*, apply pressure to the nose by pinching the nostrils together for about ten minutes. If that does not work try packing the nostrils with cotton wool and and applying ice cubes to either side of the nose.

If you have a *chest, head or abdominal wound*, keep as quiet as possible – do not touch the wound. Summon help. If you have a foreign object imbedded in you, glass in your hand, for instance, or something in your eye, do not attempt to remove it yourself, go to the nearest Accident and Emergency hospital department or doctor's surgery.

If garden chemicals go onto your skin, plunge the affected part into plain water; if your eyes are affected, plunge your face, with your eyes open, into the water. Keep doing this until any pain subsides, then cover the affected area and see your doctor.

If you start to choke on something, put your fist into the soft spot under the middle of the ribcage and keeping 'punching' yourself, or bend forwards over the back of a chair and bounce your abdomen off it. Both these actions should help to force the matter up out of the windpipe. If does not work, go out into the street and find someone to help.

If you burn or scald yourself, immediately immerse the affected part in cold water for as long as possible, or keep putting a cold, wet pad over it. Remove any tight clothing or jewellery because swelling could occur. As with bleeding, raise the affected part up so that the circulation slows down. Do not put any cream on the burn, it should be kept dry. Leave blisters alone, just loosely cover everything with a clean dry cloth and call the doctor. If you have burnt your mouth, suck ice in order to stop any swelling occurring that may constrict your airway. You should do the same should you be stung in the mouth by a bee or a wasp.

If your clothes catch fire, grab the nearest large cloth – rug, tablecloth, towel – and try to smother the fire. Hold it over you tightly and roll in it on the floor. Do not try to remove burnt material which has attached itself to your skin.

If you should faint, when you recover consciousness, do not attempt to do anything other than call your doctor or a neighbour and lay down on the bed.

HYPOTHERMIA

Although hypothermia can happen accidentally, it is essentially an insidious condition that can happen over several hours, the victim becoming sleepier and sleepier in this time and not realising that he or she is freezing to death. The elderly or disabled are particularly vulnerable, although some younger people with poor circulation can also suffer from the condition. You can avoid hypothermia by always dressing warmly in several loose layers, keeping the home as warm as possible, taking frequent warm drinks, and moving about as much as possible.

8·TAKING A BREAK

Good mental health is maintained by having an active social life, interests, variety, by freeing your home life from anxiety as much as possible, and by managing your money. The pinnacle of your well-being and efforts should be your holiday. Everyone needs a break, a change from day-to-day routine, a change from life's pressures – an escape. Being alone on holidays, though, can be a problem, even a little restricting. For example, it would not be advisable for a single woman to go on holiday alone to some of the Middle Eastern countries. Neither would it be a good idea for anyone, male or female, to hitch-hike alone across Europe. It is, however, possible to respect the limitations without totally abandoning the idea of a holiday altogether, or deciding that you can only go with a friend (which could be disastrous).

I have always enjoyed holidays alone because they allow me to do what I want to do and not what someone else wants to do. With a little research, it is possible to find some holidays where you can have the best of both worlds – companionship of people, but privacy when you want it.

THE OPTIONS

Holidays with relatives

The first option is one of not actually going on holiday alone, but going with a relative or friend. You should consider whether this is really what you want to do, or whether it is because you have never been on holiday alone before and the thought of it makes you nervous. Do you really enjoy the company of the person who is supposed to be accompanying you, or do you merely tolerate him or her because you feel you have no other choice? Do you want the kind of holiday they are willing to consider, or will you be going along with it to satisfy them?

You could be very happy if you are not putting your enjoyment in second place or you could be making the most enormous compromises because you lack the courage to go alone on the sort of holiday that you would really enjoy. Any travel agent can advise you as to what is available, but there is also a charity called the Holiday Care Service which provides free information and advice on holidays for people with special needs (see Useful Names and Addresses.) Several other charities also give advice, CRUSE, for instance, publish a guide to holidays for all ages and interests.

Freewheeling holidays

If you choose this type of holiday a good starting point is to decide on a city that fascinates you and which you have always wanted to visit and book a package trip (that is one in which travel, hotel, and meals are included, with some guided tours). I have been to Amsterdam, Bruges, Madrid, Prague, Moscow, Kiev, and several American cities this way. There is so much to see in cities – museums, shops, theatres, art galleries, parks – and you can easily walk around most city centres quite happily, as long as you remember the basic safety rules. Only the evenings can be a problem. For women alone, it is not advisable to go sightseeing at night unless it is with a guided tour of nightspots. Trips to the theatre by taxi are fine. I usually find, though, that I have done so much walking and sightseeing during the day that, by the time I have had a meal and a bath, I am quite happy to read in bed for an hour and then go to sleep.

If you want to explore further, in most cities there are plenty of guided bus tours that will take you to places of special interest outside their limits.

Singles holidays

This used to mean holidays aimed at pairing singles, but not any more. The sort of holidays available range from Club

Med, to Saga Holidays, who arrange specialist tours for people over 60, and everything in between. Some of the holidays that cater for the younger element may still be slanted towards pairing people off, but those that cater for the older age groups are not.

Special interest holidays

These present marvellous opportunities for meeting like-minded people in a friendly atmosphere. Whether the holiday is a gathering of opera buffs in Glyndebourne or a trek of vampire fans to Transylvanian castles, it is great fun because everyone has the same interest at heart. A company called Worldwide Tours produces a publication called *Special Interest Tours*, which covers holidays all over the world in categories from Adventure/Activity to Wine Tasting Festivals. Your travel agent should have a copy.

Learning holidays

Many people find great joy in combining a holiday with learning a new skill. Summer schools are usually held in country houses and the CRUSE booklet on holidays lists some of these examples:
Arvon Foundation (Devon) runs courses on poetry, fiction, playwriting, and writing for television;
Carwen House Studio (Cornwall) runs week-long landscape painting courses;
The Garden Forum (Somerset) runs gardening courses; and there are many others.

House party holidays

These gather assorted people in country houses for the purpose of rest, relaxation, and activity. Many are run by Christian organisations and operate under a friendly, welcoming philosophy. Others combine the house party with a special interest holiday, such as a gourmet weekend in a country house. House party holidays are very popular venues for single people at Christmas.

Health-based holidays

A single person can quite easily spend a week at a health farm or clinic without any feeling of loneliness or of being out-of-step with everyone else. There are health resorts both at home and abroad. Czechoslovakia has some remarkable health centres, such as Karlovy Vary (which used to be called Carlsbad) where one can take the waters and have other health treatments. There are also many, rather expensive places in Switzerland and France.

Retreats

If you want somewhere peaceful and quiet, away from work and life's pressures there are several communities that offer retreats. Some are very monastic, with the accent on contemplation and little talking, others are more lively.

Cruises

Many retired single people go on a cruise. They are a very good way of making friends and relaxing. The Americans have made a cult out of swinging singles cruises. The good thing about cruises is that you always have the ship's staff to help you if you have a problem and there are always guided tours laid on at every port of call. Neither will you feel left out of the night life, because, again, the ship's crew have special instructions to make sure that people travelling alone are always included in every activity.

Coach holidays

Some people regard coach holidays as like being carted around like sheep in a truck, but they are rather good for people travelling alone. You are always supervised by a guide and the coach driver, so no harm can befall you. The only hazard might be the person who you find yourself seated next to. However, the coaches make frequent stops for sightseeing and to stay in hotels overnight, which will allow you to escape.

Working holidays

Lots of young people have to work in their summer holidays in order to supplement a meagre college grant. For other people, who are already working, but get a certain number of weeks paid holiday a year, it's a way of enjoying a change of scenery, becoming fit, and earning some extra money. Jobs range from grape-picking in Italy to working as a tour guide abroad for English tourists. An organisation called Vacation Work International in Oxford publishes directories of summer jobs in the United Kingdom and abroad, which are available at bookshops.

Holidays for the disabled

Again, the Holiday Care Service can provide you with details of what is available and would suit your pocket. RADAR also publish a book that deals specifically with holidays for the disabled, and your local social services department will also have information and possibly funding assistance. There are almost as many varieties of holidays available for the disabled as for able-bodied people.

Special festivals

A friend of mine goes every year to the Mozart Festival in Vienna, it is her greatest pleasure. I have had the good fortune to be in Bruges when the city has had a festival and in Ghent for the same sort of thing. It is wonderful to be in a town when there is a festival on. There are street entertainments and special theatre events and the atmosphere is great. I keep promising myself every year that I will go to the Christmas Market in Nuremberg, but I never get around to it.

Holidaying at home

This is a special category of holiday that can often prove the best change or rest that you can have. If you are a very busy person, working full-time (or even more than full-time) then one or two weeks of just being at home and forgetting about work can be marvellous. After a couple of days of complete rest you can do all the things that you have been meaning to do for ages – jobs around the house; shopping for clothes; meeting friends for lunch; having day trips out to places of interest; doing the garden; sunbathing; fruit-picking at the local pick-your-own farm and filling up your freezer; writing a book you have always meant to write or painting; seeing all the shows that you are too tired to see during a working week; and so on.

Or you can do absolutely nothing but lie in the sun in the garden and tan. You could even have a do-it-yourself health farm treatment at home, by devoting your whole time to exercise, diet, sauna baths, or any of the programmes you would want from a health farm at about one-tenth of the cost.

A past employer of mine used to give himself a gourmet week at home once a year. He would go to Fortnum and Masons and buy caviar, quails eggs, and many other exotic foods, plus some very fine wines, and then luxuriated in very special meals in the sanctity of his own home.

Whatever your holiday preference, the fact that you live alone need not inhibit your ability to have great leisure breaks.

YOUR HEALTH AND SAFETY ABROAD

There are different hazards in different countries, and in this book I could not possibly cover every health and safety risk in every country of the world. A marvellous book that does is called *The Traveller's Handbook* edited by Melissa Shales and published by Heinemann. Try to find a copy if you are considering expanding your horizons.

The safety rules for life on the streets in the United Kingdom (listed in Chapter Six of this book) apply equally abroad, and you must be extra vigilant in hotels and other public places about pickpockets and thieves. Unfortunately, in tourist areas, crime can be very well organised. Put all your valuables and extra cash in the hotel safe every day, neither leave it in your room (hotel rooms are too easily broken into) nor carry it around with you. You will probably need to carry your passport and some money, so invest in a money belt that fits round your waist and has zipped compartments. Do not give your camera to a passing stranger and ask him to take a picture of you, so many times it has happened that the stranger has then run off with it. If you want to have a snapshot of yourself, see if you can find a friendly policeman to perform the task.

While you are abroad, you must be careful of your health. Only drink bottled water (a well-known brand, if possible, such as Perrier) and do not have ice in your drinks. Also, try to avoid fruit such as melon, which absorbs a great deal of water during its growth period. If you are going to a part of the world which is rife with certain diseases then investigate with your doctor beforehand as to whether you should have vaccinations. The usual vaccinations required for certain countries are cholera, typhoid, and yellow fever.

The African continent harbours Aids, Malaria, Sleeping Sickness, Lassa Fever, and many other life-threatening or incurable diseases. Be extra vigilant about what you eat or drink and with what or whom you come into contact. Do not eat too much meat, fish, or shellfish in very hot climates: you are safer eating vegetarian food during your stay.

Never go anywhere near stray cats or dogs abroad. In this country we are not accustomed to the threat of rabies; it is not the same abroad. Every country in Europe has rabies except for the United Kingdom.

If you are taken ill abroad, bear in mind that free or reduced cost emergency medical treatment is available in other European Community countries for visitors from the United Kingdom. You need to apply for an E111 form from your local DHSS office at least one month before going abroad. Keep the form with your passport as you will need it to hand if you are taken ill. The procedures for obtaining medical treatment in each country are detailed on the back of form E111. You must follow these to the letter or you may have to pay private charges. If you have health insurance, you may be covered for private treatment abroad anyway. If this is the case always take the policy with you to produce for the doctor.

PREPARING FOR YOUR HOLIDAY

The preparations for going away on holiday are the same as those outlined in Chapter Seven for going into hospital. If you have forgotten anything, you can always phone whoever has a key to your house or is looking after it for you. It is possible to telephone home, generally with ease, from most parts of the world. A list made beforehand and ticked off should obviate the necessity for this though.

Always make sure that whoever is nominally responsible for your home and its contents knows where you are going and, if you are going abroad, with which tour operator in the United Kingdom you are dealing. If there is any crisis that requires your return this will ensure that they will be able to contact you.

Packing

Take a minimum of uncrushable clothes and no more than two pairs of shoes. There is no need to weigh yourself down with excessive amounts of toiletries unless you are going to a remote area without either chemists or supermarkets. For most people a good book is a necessity when travelling; choose a paperback to keep the weight down. Leave space in your suitcase for any duty-free items, presents, or works of art that you may buy while you are away.

Transport

Organise trouble-free transport to and from the railway station, airport, or bus depot. It is not worth driving yourself to the major airports in the United Kingdom. Parking is expensive and troublesome; it is much better to put the money away for a taxi there and back, if you can. Make your travelling as free of harrassment as possible. Your holiday will have a bad start if you have to struggle with luggage, deal with train cancellations, and endure a frantic rush to reach the plane just in time. For the same reason, I suggest that you avoid overseas package tours that require you to be at the airport in the early hours of the morning, or very late at night, when you may have difficulty travelling to the airport safely.

Finally, when choosing an overseas package tour, do not skimp. Choose a good hotel, even bordering on the luxurious if you can. If there are two of you holidaying together you can cheer each other up and laugh about life's adversities and the fact that you are holidaying in a flea pit. If you are on your own in a hovel it is nothing other than miserable.

9·SHARING YOUR SPACE

This book is meant for people who live alone, so this chapter is not about sharing your living accommodation permanently, but temporarily: perhaps with a pet, which will last as long as their lifetime, perhaps with a guest or a short-term lodger. Any of these things will require some adjustment on your part, because you will have someone or something to think of, apart from yourself.

A period of sharing your home is sometimes healthy, because it teaches you to be more adaptable and stops you from becoming too set in your ways. You ought to be able to cope with a small invasion of your privacy now and then.

Keeping a pet means added responsibility, which perhaps is good, if you can cope with it. Keeping a pet is not like owning a video, though, a pet is not just something that is there for your entertainment, it is something that you have to *care* for.

KEEPING PETS

The value of non-human companions is inestimable. It has certainly been proved by the medical profession that stroking an animal lowers human blood pressure (and does a lot for the animal too). But aside from the health benefits, the joy to be derived from pets; the companionship; the interest; and, in some cases, the security, is almost beyond words.

My dog can make me laugh, shows me affection constantly, keeps me company, gives me something to cuddle and stroke, and keeps me fit. Moreover, when you have a pet, even if it is only a goldfish, it means that you never come home to an empty house.

Keeping pets, providing that you take your responsibilities very seriously, genuinely love animals, and look after the pets properly, is marvellous whether you live alone or with other people.

Choosing the right pet

The sort of pet you can keep depends very much on where you live, whether you work or are out all day, and how much money you have. Any dog really should live in a house with a garden, have at least an *accompanied* two mile walk a day, with some time off the leash in which to run around. It will cost at least £1.00 a day to feed, needs some companionship from you throughout the day, and all sorts of other commitments from you which, on consideration, you may not be prepared to make. A cat is less demanding (it does not need to be taken for walks for a start) and a fish even less so, (although some expensive tropical fish need careful temperature control and special food).

Whatever pet you choose you will also have to buy a number of accessories – leads, collars, balls, beds, cages, bells, tanks, and so on. As I mentioned in the chapter on managing money, you can take out a special pet insurance to help you cope will all the bills.

You may live in a place where pets that run around, like cats and dogs, are not allowed. Some councils are still strict about allowing tenants to keep certain pets, and most sheltered accommodation complexes, whether rented or private, are also strict about keeping pets.

You must be realistic about your age and mobility too. It is not fair to have a dog if you are unable to take it for walks – even a small lap dog. If you cannot manage to clean your house or flat every day you should not keep six cats, either, because the place will smell appalling very quickly.

You must think about the time that you have available to spend with an animal. If, literally, all the time you can spare, is five minutes in the morning before you go to work, and a couple of hours in the evening when you come home, then you would probably be better off with a caged animal, such as a hamster or bird. No pet can be ignored. All pets need feeding, clean bedding, decent living conditions and amusement. Even birds need toys – fish must have some plants and rocks to swim around.

Of course, keeping a pet, any pet, means that you cannot go on holiday without making arrangements for someone else to look after it. Pets can be a tremendous tie. I have never been able to bring myself to put my dog in kennels if I go away. I either leave her with someone that she likes and trusts, or ask someone to stay at my house and look after her. I know many other dog and cat owners who feel the same.

All in all, if you want to keep a pet, you must choose very carefully. Age Concern run an advisory service whereby they match pets up to elderly people. The RSPCA, Petwatch, or many of the other animal organisations that exist will be able to advise you about particular pets you may be interested in keeping. Your local vet will also advise you and will probably have leaflets in his or her surgery that have been published by the various pet food manufacturers.

Health

ANIMAL HEALTH Any pet will incur veterinary bills. There will be annual innoculations, medicines for various ailments, like worms and fleas, and perhaps various operations like spaying or neutering apart from any emergency fees. It can be expensive.

HUMAN HEALTH There are certain hazards to human health as well as benefits from animals. Even the cleanest of dogs can pick up worms and one of these *toxicara canis* can cause blindness in humans if they come into contact with it, therefore all dog's mess in the garden should be buried immediately. The cleanest of dogs and cats can pick up fleas, particularly if dogs go rabbiting in the woods when you let them off the leash. One flea can lay hundreds of eggs, which can infest your carpets and furniture in no time, especially if

141

you have central heating. There are sprays, powders, and shampoos for sale, of course, but it takes time and effort to deal with it. Birds can transmit the disease psitticosis to humans, while mice, rats, hamsters, gerbils, guinea pigs, and rabbits can bite clean through your finger if they feel like it.

Problems with pets

Some of the other negative aspects of keeping pets are the mess that they make. Dogs and cats shed hairs and trail mud through clean houses. Puppies will defaecate and urinate on the floor until they are house trained (which is quite a lengthy and trying process) and, when they are teething, they may chew skirting boards, the legs of your furniture, and any loose objects they can reach while you are out. Some dogs howl if they are left alone in the house and puppies will initially howl at night. Cats love to scratch the furniture (even if they have a scratching post), and some even like to climb the curtains. Any kind of rodent tends to be a nocturnal creature and may well keep you awake at night scampering about its cage. Singing canaries or talking minah birds may drive you to distraction with their singing or constant chatter.

Despite the problems, though, I would not be without a pet. Many of my friends feel the same way too. One friend of mine would much rather watch the activity in his tropical fish tank than his television; a widowed neighbour of mine found that acquiring a dog helped her to overcome the loss of her husband; a busy career woman of my acquaintance says 'Money couldn't buy the sort of welcome that I get from my cats when I get home at night.'

ANIMAL INTRUDERS

While your pets may be lovely, other people's pets, particularly cats that dig up your garden and defaecate over it, are not.

Any animal that is the property of another person is

protected under the Protection of Animals Act 1911, which makes it an offence to cause undue suffering to a domestic animal. So, much as you might like to shoot or poison nextdoor's cat, you should not even throw anything at it – except water. You can deter cats and dogs by using substances which give off smells they find unpleasant. These preparations are sold in garden centres, and come in either spray, pellet, wax, or powder form for application to plants, or to the ground.

If you have pets of your own, your garden is visited by other people's pets, or you like to encourage birds to feed in your garden, do not put bait down to kill slugs, or you will poison the animal or birdlife that you want to encourage.

Wildlife and insects

Many people are terrified of wildlife invading their gardens, but most of it is harmless, possibly slightly destructive to lawns or plants, but certainly not likely to attack humans.

Any infestation inside the house, of rats, mice, ants, cockroaches, fleas, lice, or other insects, can be dealt with for a small fee by your local council. The Environmental Health department will swiftly deal with any such human health hazard, or your can go to a private firm, such as Rentokil. Proprietory brands of substances for dealing with many of these household pests can be bought in chemists shops but, personally, I would advise calling in professionals. Putting poison down for mice may rid you of that problem, but they are likely to crawl away somewhere to die and nasty smells will then emanate from your skirting boards.

In the garden, the Environmental Health department are also empowered to deal with foxes, rats, mice, rabbits, pigeons, starlings, feral cats, and wasps nests. They will not necessarily exterminate them, but may encourage them to move on and help to proof your territory against them. With feral cats, for example, the local authority tends to neuter them because it is better to have one family of cats that cannot reproduce staking out a garden as their territory, than removing them and having another, more problematic colony move in. Foxes will not usually haunt human areas, unless they are starving and you keep leaving bits of food about. A positive aspect of their presence is that they will kill any wild mice, rats, or rabbits in your garden. If you do not want to encourage them, though, then food rubbish must not be left in easy-to-get-at plastic bags. Either put it temporarily in a strong dustbin, or lock your rubbish in a shed or garage until collection time.

Moles, hedgehogs, and badgers can be a nuisance, but they are basically harmless. Hedgehogs will benefit your garden by eating all your slugs. Badgers, unfortunately, will make straight for your blackberries, as they love them. Moles, of course, will make unsightly mounds in your lawn.

You cannot do anything about badgers, as they are protected by law, you will just have to wait for them to move on. But moles can be deterred. Any plant from the onion family – onion, garlic or leek produces a smell which is supposed to deter moles. Plant these in between your prize roses. You can also sink slates or paving stones at intervals along your flower beds. They will stop moles burrowing along and uprooting your best plants. Another method of deterring them is to plant empty glass bottles along the edge of flower beds, with the necks exposed. The noise made when the wind blows across the top of the bottles unnerves moles, who have very sensitive hearing. The RSPCA is a good source of advice, it has produced some very useful booklets on moles, foxes, badgers, and hedgehogs.

The Wildlife and Countryside Act 1981 gives total protection to certain endangered species and limits the methods of extermination used for others. For example, bats, certain butterflies, crickets, moths, and dragonflies are protected as are the great crested newt, the natterjack toad, and the red squirrel. If you think that any of these are inhabiting your garden, call your local conservation group (the phone number will be in your library) and they will send an expert.

If you have an uncovered fishpond, you are likely to attract herons, kingfishers and seagulls. You may appreciate seeing them, but they are expert at taking fish.

HAVING VISITORS

BEFORE THE VISIT Chapter Five of this book discusses the questions of food and drink. If anyone has an allergy which requires a special diet, it is best if they bring their special food with them, as you may not be able to obtain it. Find out if there are any particular sleeping arrangements to be made: whether they need a board under the bed (which they cannot be expected to bring with them), or may have to have your bedroom because it is nearer the toilet.

Thoroughly clean the place and do as many as possible of the regular household chores before your guest arrives so that as little as possible has to be done during the visit.

Plan some visits to places of interest, shopping trips or visits to the local theatre. Conversation quickly runs out if you spend all the time within the same four walls and you are both more likely to wish the visit would end quickly.

Make sure that when the guest's visit is arranged you agree upon a specific start and finish date and time. It is very inconvenient and does not help you relax and enjoy the company of your guest if you do not know when he or she will either arrive or depart.

DURING THE VISIT The visit is going to be disruptive to your usual pattern of things and your guest may have habits that irritate you, so the best thing to do is to relax and accept it. There is no point in ruining a lifelong friendship because your guest does not squeeze the toothpaste tube in the same place you always do. Accept the fact that you may have to clear up after your guest, who may leave the bathroom in a mess and certainly will not know where you put everything in the kitchen. Tell them to make themselves properly at home and, if they are up before you are, to make themselves a cup of tea and not feel awkward about it. Show them where everything is so that if you are out they can cope.

You will probably have to cancel a certain amount of your usual social activities while you have a guest staying with you, but do not cancel all of them. If you usually visit an activity club once a week, take your guest with you. If you are a pensioner and you usually go to your local day centre or 'pop-in' club, and your guest is of similar age, ask if they would like to accompany you.

The fact that you have a guest is something to enjoy and make use of. It provides you with the opportunity to do all the things that you have wanted to do but have been unable to do on your own. While you have another pair of hands in the house you can move heavy pieces of furniture, decorate the living room, perhaps help with any clothes' alteration that is difficult or impossible on your own, such as pinning up hems of trousers or dresses, and so on. If you have such activities in mind make sure your guest knows that he or she is going to have to do some work during the visit; anyone coming for a complete rest might be a little taken aback otherwise.

I would advise that you do not, if you are working, use up all your holiday time entertaining guests. It is important that you have some time to yourself and have a complete rest. Looking after the needs of a guest, no matter how relaxed you feel with them, is not a rest. On the other hand, you should not feel that you are too elderly or too disabled to have a guest. Organisations such as the Red Cross, the WRVS and the social services will all help you to cope by providing extra equipment for a weekend, extra meals on wheels, or transport.

Temporary lodgers

You may find it necessary to take in a lodger because you are short of cash, or to help a friend who has been made homeless. Either way, do not do it unless you have a house or flat that allows for a certain amount of self-containment – ideally, you would have two bathrooms and can provide the person with their own room, in which they can do some cooking if necessary. You may not be at all happy if you have to share everything that you have been used to having to yourself. You must have some privacy and so must they and therefore the temporary lodger must live in his or her own quarters, not in yours.

No matter how well you know the person, do not be casual about the arrangement. Take legal advice and draw up a proper tenancy agreement with carefully defined rules about what the lodger may or may not do, how much the rent is to be and when it is payable, and how long the tenancy period is to last. Otherwise you may have problems in making them go if you cannot show that they have contravened a written agreement or that the agreed term of tenancy has expired. Always give the person a rent book or give them receipts, and keep a record yourself of all financial transactions. Make sure that the rent that you set covers everything that is necessary – light, heat, water, etc. Put a lock on the telephone so that they may only use it with your permission and so that you can log the call and exact the right amount of money for it.

Taking in a lodger is fraught with problems, whether it is a friend or a stranger. Friends think that they can take all sorts of liberties, such as not paying the rent for a week, having other friends in late at night and leaving the place in a mess. Strangers can be even more of a problem, because you really do not know anything about them and take them in on trust. Ask for references from the applicant's bank manager or employer, and check them.

You may be able to have a part-time lodger. For instance you may find someone who works away from home and would like to rent your second bedroom during the week, but will be going home every weekend. Alternatively you might consider renting to students from a local college who will only be in your house during term time. Be prepared for some lodgers, such as nurses, to be working irregular hours.

If you consider taking lodgers the main thing is to be certain it is what you want to do and that you have fully researched the pros and cons of the situation.

Your life is your own when you live alone. You do not have to bend to the demands and whims of others. You do not have to share your food, your wardrobe, your garden, or your time with anyone else. You may wish that you did. You may long for the right life-partner to come along. But, whether it is for now or forever, resolve to enjoy your life alone and derive as much out of it as you can.

Useful Names and Addresses

ABTA – The Association of British Travel Agents Limited
55–57 Newman Street
London W1P 4AH
Advice on holidays and travel in general

Age Concern
Bernard Sunley House
60 Pitcairn Road
Mitcham
Surrey CR4 3LL
Advice and practical help for the elderly

Alcoholics Anonymous
11 Redcliffe Gardens
London SW10
Help for anyone with a drink problem

Association of British Insurers
Aldermary House
10–15 Queen Street
London EC4 1TT
Advice on insurance and home security

Banking Information Service
10 Lombard Street
London EC3V 9AR
Literature about banking services

British Red Cross Society
9 Grosvenor Crescent
London SW1X 7EJ
Source of aid and temporary appliances for elderly and disabled

British Security Industry Association Ltd
Scorpio House
102 Sydney Street
London SW3 6NL
Lists of approved security equipment manufacturers

The Building Societies' Association
3 Savile Row
London W1X 1AF
Information about home buying and borrowing money

Citizens' Advice Bureau
National Office
115–123 Pentonville Road
London N1 9LZ
Practical help and advice across a wide range of legal and domestic problems

Consumers' Association
PO Box 44
Hertford SG14 1SH
Advice and literature on consumer matters

Counsel and Care for the Elderly
Tyman House,
Lower Ground Floor
16 Bonny Street
Camden
London NW1 9PG
Advice and help for the elderly

CRUSE
Cruse House
126 Sheen Road
Richmond

Surrey TW9 1UR
Advice, help and publications for the widowed

Disability Alliance Educational & Research Association
25 Denmark Street
London WC2 8NJ
Advice and literature for the disabled

Disabled Living Foundation
380–384 Harrow Road
London W9 2HU
Information on aids for disabled people

Disablement Income Group
Millmead Business Centre
Millmead Road
London N17 9QU
Money advice for disabled people

Distressed Gentlefolk's Aid Association
Vicarage Gate House
Vicarage Gate
Kensington
London W8 4AQ

Fire Protection Association
140 Aldersgate Street
London EC1A 4HX
Advice and literature on fire prevention

Glass and Glazing Federation
44–48 Borough High Street
London SE1 1XB
Advice on all aspects of double glazing and safety glass

Help the Aged
St James' Walk
London EC1R OBE
Advice and help for the elderly

Holiday Care Service
2 Old Bank Chambers
Station Road
Horley
Surrey RH6 9HW

Advice on holidays for those with special needs

Housing Corporation
Maple House
149 Tottenham Court Road
London W1P OBW
Advice on public housing and sources of government aid

Independent Association of Alarm Installers
2 Command Road
South Gosforth
Newcastle Upon Tyne
List of approved installers

Law Centre Federation
Duchess House
18–19 Warren Street
London W1P 5DB
List of local law centres where free legal advice is given

Law Society
113 Chancery Lane
London WC2A 1PL
Advice and complaints against the legal profession

The Mental After Care Association
110 Jermyn Street
London SW1Y 6HB
Support for those recovering from mental illness

MIND – National Association of Mental Health
22 Harley Street
London W1N 2ED
Advice and help for the mentally ill

Money Advice Centre
The Birmingham Settlement
318 Summerlane
Birmingham B19
Advice on all money matters

National Association of Estate Agents
Arbon House
21 Jury Street

Warwick CV34 4EH
Advice on home buying and using estate agents

National Association of Victim Support Schemes
17a Electric Lane
London SW9 8LA
Help and advice for victims of crime

National Association for Widows
Chell Road
Stafford ST16 2QA
Advice for the widowed

National Council of Women of Great Britain
36 Danbury Street
Islington
London N1 8JU
Advice and support for women living alone

National Supervisory Council for Intruder Alarms
14 Cookham Road
Maidenhead
Berks SL6 8AJ
List of approved manufacturers and installers

New Homes' Marketing Board
82 New Cavendish Street
London WIM 8AD
Information on new homes for sale thoughout the UK

RADAR – Royal Association for Disability and Rehabilitation
25 Mortimer Street
London W1N 8AB
Advice and literature for the disabled

RELATE – National Marriage Guidance Council
Herbert Gray College
Little Church Street
Rugby
Warwicks CV21 3AP
Advice and help with any personal

relationship, not just marriage, and literature on coping alone

RELEASE
169 Commercial Street
London E1 6BW
Advice on legal, criminal and drug-related problems

RoSPA – Royal Society for the Prevention of Accidents
Cannon House
The Priory
Queensway
Birmingham B4 6BS
Advice on accident prevention in the home

RSPCA – Royal Society for the Prevention of Cruelty to Animals
The Causeway
Horsham
West Sussex RH12 1HG
Advice about pets and practical help with wildlife

The Salvation Army
101 Queen Victoria Street
London EC4P 4EP
Practical support and centres for the lonely

SHAC – Shelter Housing Aid Centre
189A Old Brompton Road
SW5 0AR
Help for the homeless

Widows' Advisory Service
Chell Road
Stafford Street
ST16 2QA
Advice for the widowed

WRVS – Womens' Royal Voluntary Service
17 Old Park Lane
London W1Y 4AJ
Practical help for the lonely, housebound and elderly

Useful Leaflets

YOUR HOME

Buying and renting a home

Alliance–Leicester Building Society
Homebuyers' Guide

Bradford & Bingley Building Society
Startline – Home Purchase Loan

The Building Societies Association
Starting Point – A Building Society Guide to House Purchase

Coventry Building Society
Homebuyers' Guide – A Home of Your Own

Department of the Environment
Housing Association Rents
Letting Rooms in Your Home
Letting Your Home or Retirement Home
Mobile Homes
Notice to Quit
The Rent Acts and You
Right to Repair
Service Charges in Flats
Shared Ownership
Shorthold Reform
The Tenants' Charter

Halifax Building Society
Buying and Selling Your Home

Leeds Permanent Building Society
First Home – A Guide for First Time Buyers

London Borough of Camden
Private Tenants – Rights During Repairs

Nationwide Anglia
Homemaker – The Homemaker's Handbook

National Association of Estate Agents
On Show to Sell
Planning to Sell a Property?
Thinking of Letting a Property?

Royal Life Insurance Ltd
Buying Your Own Home

Woolwich Equitable Building Society
The Woolwich Step-By-Step Guide to Buying Your First Home

Energy management

Age Concern
Warmth In Winter

Association of British Insurers
Watch Out for Winter

The Electricity Council
Electric Blankets
Flexes and Cables
A Guide to Running Costs
How to Make Your Home Energy Wise with Economy 7
How to Read your Meter
Plugs and Fuses
Using Energy Wisely
Warmth Without Waste

Department of the Environment
All about Loft, Tank and Pipe Insulation

Halifax Building Society
Conserving Energy in the Home

Seeboard
Compare the Cost of Home Heating
Complete Guide to Electricity
Double Glazing – the Natural Way to Improve your Home

Easy Ways of Paying for Electricity
Home Insulation – Cut the Cost of Heating your Home
Prices for Electricity Used in the Home

Safety and security

Abbey National Building Society
A Guide to Home Security

Central Office of Information
Danger from Fire
How to Protect Your Home

Halifax Building Society
Home Security and Insurance
Safety Measures in Your Home

RoSPA
Fire Safety for Disabled Living
The Home Safety Book
How to Avoid Falls
Safety on a Shoestring

Seeboard
How to Provide Protection in Your Home
Is Danger Lurking in Your Home
Put Your Wiring on Trial
Security Systems

Improving the Home; Decorating; Gardening

Halifax Building Society
Guide to Decorating your Home
Making Improvements to your House
Making the Most of your Garden

LOOKING AFTER YOURSELF

Health
Bloomsbury Health Education Department
Aim for Health

The Flora Project for Heart Disease Prevention
Fitness & Exercise
Stress

The Health Education Authority
Exercise. Why Bother?
A Guide to Examining Your Breasts
A Guide to Healthy Eating
A Guide to Sensible Drinking

Ministry of Agriculture
Look at the Label

Loneliness and Depression

CRUSE
By Myself – The Experience of Loneliness
Depression – What It Is and What To Do About it
Early Days in Widowhood
The First Year – A Widow Looks Back
Helping the Widowed
Household Guide for Widowers
How to Worry Usefully

CU Life Assurance
Coping on Your Own

Department of Health and Social Security
What to do After a Death

Halifax Building Society
Home Help for Widows
A New Start – Making the Best of Redundancy

MIND
Agoraphobia and Other Phobias
Anxiety
Depression
Talking Treatments

National Marriage Guidance Council
Alone Again

The Samaritans
Everybody Needs Someone

Elderly and Disabled

Age Concern
Advice for Elderly People – Electricity and You

Council and Care
Accommodation for People over Retirement Age

Halifax Building Society
Special Schemes for the Retired and Elderly
Solving the Retirement Money Puzzle

Social Security

Department of Health and Social Security
Housing Benefit
Income Support – Cash Help
Social Security Benefit Rates
   Attendance Allowance (Leaflet NI205)
   Child Benefit (CH1)
   Christmas Bonus (NI229)
   Family Credit (NI261)
   Guardian's Allowance (NI14)
   Hospital Rates (NI9)
   Housing Benefit (RR1)
   Income Support (SB1)
   Industrial Death Benefit (NI10)
   Industrial Injuries & Disablement Benefit (NI6)
   Invalid Care Allowance (ICA) (NI212)
   Invalidity Benefit (NI16A)
   Maternity Allowance (NI17A)
   Mobility Allowance (NI211)
   NHS Benefits (AB11)
   One Parent Benefit (CH11)
   Pneumoconiosis, Byssinosis and Miscellaneous Diseases Benefit Scheme (PN1)
   Retirement Pension (NP32) or (NP46)
   Severe Disablement Allowance (SDA) (NI252)
   Sickness Benefit (NI16)
   Social Fund (SB16)
   Statutory Maternity Pay (NI17A)
   Statutory Sick Pay (NI244)
   Unemployment Benefit (NI12)
   War Pensions (MPL152) and (MPL153)
   Widow's Benefits (NP45)
   Workmen's Compensation Supplement (WS1)

Holidays and social activities

CRUSE
Holidays

DHSS for United Kingdom Health Departments
Protect Your Health Abroad

DHSS and Central Office of Information
Medical Costs Abroad

Holiday Care Service
Singles Holidays

Young people and students

Halifax Building Society
Making the Most of Student Life

Midland Bank
Into Your First Year

MANAGING MONEY

Budgeting

Midland Bank
How To Budget

Tax

The Alexander Consulting Group
Inheritance Tax
Unit Trusts

The Inland Revenue
Age Allowance
Income Tax and Pensioners
Income Tax and School Leavers
Income Tax and Strikes
*Income Tax Lay-offs and
    Short-time Work*
Income Tax and the Unemployed
Income Tax and Widows

Price Waterhouse
The Pocket Tax Book

Mortgages/Conveyancing

Abbey National Building Society
Complete Mortgage Guide
Mortgage Facts & Figures
Repayment Mortgage

Confederation Mortgage Services
*Choose Your Mortgage as
    Carefully as You Choose Your
    Home*

Fourmat Publishing
*Conveyancing – Fees and Duties
    on Sale of Freehold*

**The Leeds Permanent Building
Society**
Calculation of Mortgage Interest
A Guide to Mortgage Payments
The APR on Your Mortgage

Lombard Continental Insurance
General Information for Vendors

Nationwide Anglia
*Facts & Figures About Your
    Mortgage*
*Homemaker – Buying Your First
    Home*

The Royal Bank of Scotland
Mortgages

**Woolwich Equitable Building
Society**
The Road to Home Ownership

Insurance

The Alexander Consulting Group
Writing a Policy in Trust

Fidelity Investment Service Ltd
*Looking Ahead – The Fidelity
    Guide to Retirement Planning*

**Office of Fair Trading and Central
Office of Information**
*It Might Never Happen but ... A
    Guide to Household Insurance*

Royal Insurance (UK) Ltd
Protect Your Home

Royal Life Ltd
Design for Living

Seeboard
New Appliance Care Plan

Sun Alliance Insurance Group
Home Insurance

Debt

Midland Bank
How to Cope with Debt

Useful Books

COMBATTING ANXIETY AND DEPRESSION

Fink, D.H., *Release from Nervous Tension*, Allen & Unwin, 1985
Frampton, M., *Agoraphobia*, Thorsons, 1984
Hauck, P., *Calm Down*, Sheldon Press, 1980
Lake, A., *How to Cope with Your Nerves*, Sheldon Press, 1988
Lambley, P., *Insomnia and Other Sleeping Problems*, Sphere, 1984
Mackarness, R., *Not All in the Mind*, Pan, 1976
Madders, J., *Stress and Relaxation*, Macdonald, 1985
Melville, J., *The Tranquilliser Trap – and How to Get Out of It*, Fontana, 1984
Miller, W. and Munoz, R., *How to Control Your Drinking*, Sheldon Press, 1983
Neville, A., *Who's Afraid of Agoraphobia*, Century Arrow, 1986
Nicol, R., *Sleep Like a Dream – The Drug-free Way*, Sheldon Press, 1988
Priest, R., *Anxiety and Depression*, Macdonald, 1985
Rowe, D., *Depression – The Way Out of Your Prison*, Routledge & Kegan Paul, 1983
Trickett, S., *Coming off Tranquillizers*, Thorsons, 1986
Weekes, C., *Self-help for your Nerves*, Angus & Robertson, 1972
Weekes, C., *Peace from Nervous Suffering*, Angus & Robertson, 1972
Weekes, C., *More Help for your Nerves*, Angus & Robertson, 1984

BEREAVEMENT AND DIVORCE

Black, J., *Divorce: The Things You Thought You'd Never Need to Know*, Paperfronts, 1982
Consumers' Association, *What To Do When Someone Dies* (revised annually)
Harper, W.M., *Divorce and Your Money*, Allen and Unwin, 1985
Hemer, J. and Stanyer, A., *Survival Guide for Widows*, Age Concern, 1986
Search, G., *Surviving Divorce: A Handbook for Men*, New English Library, 1985
Shapiro, J., *On Your Own: a Guide to Independent Living*, Pandora Press, 1985
Tatelbaum, J., *The Courage to Grieve*, Heinemann, 1981
Williams, A., *Alone Again*, Relate (National Marriage Guidance Council), 1977
Wylie, B.J., *Beginnings: A Book for Widows*, Unwins, 1986

RETIREMENT

Age Concern, *Heating Help in Retirement*, Age Concern, 1984
Age Concern, *The Elderly Shopper* (Age Concern Working Party Report), 1985
Age Concern, *Your Rights 1987*, Age Concern, 1987
Age Concern and the National Housing and Town Planning Council, *Owning Your Home in Retirement*, Age Concern, 1987
Muir Gray, J.A., *Gardening in Retirement*, Age Concern, 1985
Pays, I., *What Every Woman Should Know About Retirement*, Age Concern, 1987
Stoppard, M., *The Prime of Your Life*, Dorling Kindersley, 1983

MONEY

Age Concern, *Your Taxes and Savings*, Age Concern, 1988
Andrews, A. and Houghton, P., *How to Cope with Credit and Deal with Debt*, Allen and Unwin, 1986
Consumers' Association, *Cutting Your Cost of Living*, Consumers' Association, 1986
Consumers' Association, *Raising the Money to Buy Your Own Home*, Consumers' Association, 1986
CPAG, *National Welfare Benefits Handbook*, CPAG, revised annually
Hetherington, T., *How to Split Up and Survive Financially*, Allen and Unwin, 1986
McQueen, J., *What to do When Someone has Debt Problems*, Paperfronts, 1985
Williams, J. and Williams, S., *Lloyds Bank Tax Guide*, Penguin, 1988

DISABILITY

Darnbrough, A. and Kinrade, D., *Directory for the Disabled*, Woodhead Faulkner, 1984
Jay, P., *Coping with Disability*, Disabled Living Foundation, 1984

HOUSING AND THE HOME

Age Concern, *Sheltered Housing for Older People* (Age Concern Working Party Report), 1984
Age Concern and the National Housing and Town Planning Council, *A Buyer's Guide to Sheltered Housing*, Age Concern, 1988
Bookbinder, D., *Housing Options for Older People*, Age Concern, 1988
Conacher, G. (ed.), *Kitchen Sense for Disabled People*, Croom Helm and the Disabled Living Foundation, 1986

Consumers' Association, *Securing Your Home*, Consumers' Association, 1982

Consumers' Association, *Dealing with Household Emergencies*, Consumers' Association, 1984

Consumers' Association, *Householders' Action Guide*, Consumers' Association, 1984

Consumers' Association, *Which Way to Buy, Sell and Move House*, Consumers' Association, 1988

Foott, S., *Handicapped at Home*, The Design Council, 1985

Hinton, C., *Using your Home as Capital*, Age Concern, 1988

SHAC, *Housing Rights Guide*, Shelter Housing Aid Centre (revised annually)

Triani, R., *Home Security and Protection*, Willow Books, 1984

EATING

Age Concern, *Eating Well on a Budget*, Age Concern, 1987

Norwak, M., *Beginner's Guide to Home Freezing*, Pelham Books, 1973

Page, D., *Slow Cooking Properly Explained*, Paperfronts, 1979

Smith, D., *One is Fun*, Hodder and Stoughton, 1985

GENERAL BOOKS

Age Concern, *Calling for Help*, Age Concern and the Research Institute for Consumer Affairs and *Which?* magazine, 1987

Conran, S., *Superwoman*, Sidgwick & Jackson, 1975 and 1977

Drake, A. (ed.), *The Personal Security Handbook*, Guild Publishing, 1987

Eisenberg, R. and Kelly, K., *Organise Yourself*, Guild Publishing, 1986

Mills, S., *Handywoman*, Corgi, 1982

National Council for Voluntary Organisations, *The Voluntary Agencies Directory* (revised annually)

Shales, M. (ed.), *The Traveller's Handbook*, Heinemann, 1985

Vacation Work International, *Directory of Summer Jobs in the UK* (revised annually)

Vacation Work International, *Directory of Summer Jobs Abroad* (revised annually)

Yates, M., *Coping – a Survival Manual for Women Alone*, Spectrum, 1976

Index

accidents 51–8, 125–8
see also first aid
Age Concern 14, 71, 141
anxiety, see health

banks, see financial institutions
bathrooms 26, 30, 31, 56–7, 75
bereavement 12, 13, 28
bills, payment of 83–4, 88, 89, 90, 91
see also electricity, gas, heating,
money, telephone
budgeting 67, 76–83, 107
building societies, see financial institutions

car 20, 23–4, 34, 77, 79, 86, 89, 90, 108
see also transport
Citizens' Advice Bureau 71, 92
cooking 65, 94–5
see also food, safety
CRUSE 8, 14, 71, 131, 132
CVS (Council of Voluntary Service) 64,
111, 122

debt 90–92
decorating 64–5, 146
depression, see health
DHSS 15, 51, 57, 64, 71–5
see also social security benefits
disabled, the
choosing a flat 31
holidays 134
and independence 12
meals on wheels 75, 96–7
personal safety 108
social security benefits 15, 64, 65,
72–4, 76–7, 92, 146
doctors 13, 25, 54, 121–2, 124, 125, 128
doors 31, 32, 49, 50, 51, 59–60
drink 65, 77, 78
and health 117
drugs 13, 120–121, 124
elderly, the
choice of house 34–5
choice of house location 25, 27, 28,
29
cooking 94
day classes 111
holidays 132
managing money 80, 92

meals on wheels 75, 96–7
personal safety 108
'pop–in parlours' 111, 146
sheltered housing 54–5
social security benefits 51, 65, 72, 76
voluntary help 64
see also retirement, social security
benefits
electricity 32, 38, 47, 91
bill 43, 77, 78, 79
electrical applicances 32, 53, 54, 56,
57, 65, 87, 91, 95, 100–101
safety 53
entertaining 95, 98, 101–4, 105–6

financial institutions 14–15, 25, 41,
83–4
banks 25, 39, 44, 68, 83, 88–90, 91
building societies 15, 39–40, 44, 68,
88–90, 91
see also post office
fire (risk and prevention) 30, 51–4
see also first aid
first aid 125–9
flat 7, 28–9
ground rent 35, 77
leasehold 35
security 7, 28–9
service charges 34, 38, 77
see also house, renting
food 45, 77, 78, 80, 94, 125
equipment 100–101
freezing 95–7, 99, 101
fresh produce 99
and health 116–118
storage 97–9
see also cooking
friends 12, 14, 16, 18–19, 20, 33, 44, 64,
67, 91–2, 105–6, 123, 125, 130–1, 135
making friends 109–114
see also guests
furniture 46, 53, 57, 62, 63, 77

garden 28, 33, 34, 45, 48, 49, 58, 124
pests 143–4
gas 32, 38, 47, 91, 123
bill 43, 77, 78, 79
leak 53
guests 95, 101–2, 145–6

health 116–125
  abroad 135–7
  mental health 18, 19, 130
    depression 11, 15, 17, 18, 29, 66, 119, 120, 124
    anxiety 11, 18–19, 21, 47, 81, 90, 106, 117, 119, 124, 130
    see also doctor, hospitals,
illness, mental health
heating 37, 52–3, 57, 77, 80, 82, 123
  see also electricity, gas
holidays 48, 123, 130–138
hospitals 24, 25, 86, 128
  convalescence 124–5
  hospitalisation 122–5
house
  buying 39–43
  choice of area 23–7
  location 7, 23–4
  moving 22, 43–6
  pests 143–4
  search 32, 41, 42
  security 7, 28–30, 32, 33, 34, 48–51
  survey 29, 40
  viewing 30–33
    see also renting

illness 25, 121–3
  see also health, social security benefits
insulation 60–62
insurance 44, 84–7
  accident 86
  buildings 77, 78, 79, 84
  car 77, 79, 85–6, 90
  contents 77, 78, 79, 84–5
  health 77, 78, 79, 86, 125
  life 85
  maisonette indemnity 85
  other 87
  travel 87

kitchens 26, 30, 31, 52, 55–6, 126

letting, see subletting
living rooms 30, 32
locks, see doors, security, windows
lodgers, see subletting

MIND 15, 18
money 67–92
  see also bills, budgeting, financial institutions, house buying
mortgage 77, 79, 80, 91
  mortgage indemnity insurance 84, 91
  mortgage protection policy 91
  see also house, buying
moving house 22, 43–6

National Insurance 71–2, 74
neighbours 12, 32, 33–4, 35, 44, 48, 49, 55, 64, 83, 88, 91–2, 105, 106, 122–3, 124, 125, 126–7
  Neighbourhood Watch scheme 49

organising, see planning

pension 68, 73, 74–5, 76, 77
pets 36, 45, 83, 122, 123, 139–43
  health 141
plants 63–4, 83, 122, 124, 125
police 7, 25, 27, 48, 107, 108
post office 25, 44, 83, 88, 89

rates 20, 77, 78, 79, 91
Red Cross 125, 146
relaxing 65, 121, 135, 144
  see also holidays
renting 27, 29, 36–8, 81
  see also flat, house
retirement 22–3, 26, 37
roofs 33, 49, 75
  see also insulation
RSPCA 141, 144

safety 30, 51–8
  personal 27, 47–8, 107–9, 114
    see also security, fire
security 27, 47–51
  see also house, safety
shopping 19, 45, 89, 95, 101, 102, 109, 122, 125, 135
  shops 24, 25, 48
social life 16–17, 18, 109–114
  see also entertaining, friends
social security benefits 15, 51, 65, 71–5, 76, 92
solicitor 34, 39, 41
  see also fees, house buying
students 12, 22, 23, 24, 25, 64, 69, 76, 92, 94, 111
  see also young people
subletting 37, 38, 69, 76, 81, 146–7
surveyor, see house survey

tax 67–71
telephone 55
  bill 43, 77, 78, 79, 82
television 20, 49, 65, 77, 78, 79, 82, 125
tenancy 36–8
transport 7, 23, 24–5, 146
  see also car

walls
  exterior 33, 50
  interior 32, 61–2
water 32, 38, 43, 60–61, 77, 78, 79, 91, 123
windows 31, 48, 49, 50, 51, 58–9
WRVS 76, 146